SINCERITY
AND AUTHENTICITY

The Charles Eliot Norton Lectures, 1969–1970

LIONEL TRILLING

SINCERITY
AND AUTHENTICITY

HARVARD UNIVERSITY PRESS

CAMBRIDGE, MASSACHUSETTS

LONDON, ENGLAND

Library of Congress Catalog Card Number 72-83468

ISBN 0-674-80861-4

PRINTED IN THE UNITED STATES OF AMERICA

To my cousin
I. BERNARD COHEN

PREFACE

These are the lectures I gave at Harvard University in the spring of 1970 as the Charles Eliot Norton Professor of Poetry. When I chose as their subject the cognate ideals of sincerity and authenticity historically considered, I could not fail to be aware that no six lectures could conceivably encompass it. This encouraged me in the undertaking. By the time I gave the last of the lectures, my consciousness that they must inevitably be inadequate had by no means diminished, but it had ceased to be inspiriting through having become specific—I knew by how much they fell short and in what particular ways, and I was anything but heartened when I enumerated the important issues and figures they did not take into account. Now that I come to publish them, substantially although not exactly as they were given, I naturally return to the thought that the subject is so very large, virtually coextensive with the culture of four centuries, that even a merely partial investigation of it might be of some use in suggesting its extent and in remarking a few of the many ironies it generates.

L. T.

New York
March 1972

CONTENTS

SINCERITY
AND AUTHENTICITY

I · SINCERITY: ITS ORIGIN AND RISE

i

Now AND THEN IT IS POSSIBLE TO OBSERVE the moral life in process of revising itself, perhaps by reduc‑ ing the emphasis it formerly placed upon one or another of its elements, perhaps by inventing and adding to itself a new element, some mode of conduct or of feeling which hitherto it had not regarded as essential to virtue.

The news of such an event is often received with a degree of irony or some other sign of resistance. Nowadays, of course, we are all of us trained to believe that the moral life is in ceaseless flux and that the values, as we call them, of one epoch are not those of another. We even find it easy to believe that the changes do not always come about gradually but are sometimes quite sudden. This ready recognition of change in the moral life is implicit in our modern way of thinking about literature. Yet sometimes it is just our ex‑ perience of literature that leads us to resist the idea of moral mutation, to question whether the observed shifts in moral assumption deserve the credence we are impelled to give them. Generally our awareness of the differences between the moral assumptions of one culture and those of another is so developed and active that we find it hard to believe there is any such thing as an essential human nature; but we all know moments when these differences, as literature attests to them, seem to make no difference, seem scarcely to

exist. We read the *Iliad* or the plays of Sophocles or Shakespeare and they come so close to our hearts and minds that
they put to rout, or into abeyance, our instructed consciousness of the moral life as it is conditioned by a particular
culture—they persuade us that human nature never varies,
that the moral life is unitary and its terms perennial, and
that only a busy intruding pedantry could ever have suggested otherwise.

And then yet again, on still another view of the case, this
judgement reverses itself and we find ourselves noting with
eager attention all the details of assumption, thought, and
behaviour that distinguish the morality of one age from that
of another, and it seems to us that a quick and informed
awareness of the differences among moral idioms is of the
very essence of a proper response to literature.

This ambivalence I describe is my own as I propose the
idea that at a certain point in its history the moral life of
Europe added to itself a new element, the state or quality of
the self which we call sincerity.

The word as we now use it refers primarily to a congruence between avowal and actual feeling. Is it really possible,
does it make sense, to say that the value put upon this
congruence became, at a given moment in history, a new
element of the moral life? Surely it is as old as speech
and gesture?

But I subdue this scepticism by reflecting that the word
cannot be applied to a person without regard to his cultural circumstances. For example, we cannot say of the
patriarch Abraham that he was a sincere man. That statement must seem only comical. The sincerity of Achilles or
Beowulf cannot be discussed: they neither have nor lack
sincerity. But if we ask whether young Werther is really as
sincere as he intends to be, or which of the two Dashwood
sisters, Elinor or Marianne, is thought by Jane Austen to be

the more truly sincere, we can confidently expect a serious response in the form of opinions on both sides of the question.

There is a moment in *Hamlet* which has a unique and touching charm. Polonius is speeding Laertes on his way to Paris with paternal advice that has scarcely the hope of being heard, let alone heeded. The old man's maxims compete with one another in prudence and dullness and we take them to be precisely characteristic of a spirit that is not only senile but small. But then we are startled to hear

> This above all: to thine own self be true
> And it doth follow, as the night the day,
> Thou canst not then be false to any man.

We naturally try to understand that concluding sentence of Polonius's speech in a way that will make it consort with our low opinion of the speaker—'If you always make your own interests paramount, if you look out for Number One, you will not mislead your associates to count on your attachment to their interests, and in this way you will avoid incurring their anger when, as is inevitable, you disappoint their expectations.' But the sentence will not submit to this reading. Our impulse to make its sense consistent with our general view of Polonius is defeated by the way the lines sound, by their lucid moral lyricism. This persuades us that Polonius has had a moment of self-transcendence, of grace and truth. He has conceived of sincerity as an essential condition of virtue and has discovered how it is to be attained.

The extent to which *Hamlet* is suffused by the theme of sincerity is part of everyone's understanding of the play. It is definitive of Hamlet himself that in his first full speech he affirms his sincerity, saying that he knows not 'seems': there is indeed a discrepancy between his avowal of feeling over his father's death and what he actually feels, but it is not the one which, as he chooses to think, his mother is attributing to him—he feels not less but more than he avows, he has that within which passeth show. The scene with the players is concerned with the artistic means by which the congruence between feeling and avowal can be effected, and this histrionic congruence is incongruously invoked by Hamlet as he stands in Ophelia's grave, outtopping Laertes in the expression of grief: 'Nay, an thou'lt mouth, / I'll rant as well as thou.' And then there is Horatio: Hamlet holds him in his heart's core because, as he says, this friend is not passion's slave; his Stoic *apatheia* makes Horatio what we feel him to be, a mind wholly at one with itself, an instance of sincerity unqualified.

But of all the elements of the play, so many more than I mention, which lead us to think about sincerity, Polonius's utterance of the famous three lines is the most engaging, perhaps because of its implicit pathos. 'To thine own self be true'—with what a promise the phrase sings in our ears! Each one of us is the subject of that imperative and we think of the many difficulties and doubts which would be settled if only we obeyed it. What a concord is proposed—between me and my own self: were ever two beings better suited to each other? Who would not wish to be true to his own self? True, which is to say loyal, never wavering in constancy. True, which is to say honest: there are to be no subterfuges in dealing with him. True, which is to say, as carpenters and bricklayers use the word, precisely aligned with him. But it is not easy. 'Why is it,' Charles Dickens wrote in a letter at the height of his career, 'that . . . a sense comes always crushing on me now, when I fall into low spirits, as of one happiness I have missed in life, and one friend and companion I have never made?' We know who that unattained friend and companion is. We understand with

Matthew Arnold how hard it is to discern one's own self
in order to reach it and be true to it.

> Below the surface-stream, shallow and light,
> Of what we *say* we feel—below the stream,
> As light, of what we *think* we feel—there flows
> With noiseless current strong, obscure and deep,
> The central stream of what we feel indeed.

It was some thirty years after Arnold's wistful statement
of the difficulty, perhaps even the impossibility, of locating
the own self that Sigmund Freud took the first steps towards
devising a laborious discipline of research to discover where
it might be found. But we are still puzzled to know not
only the locus of the self to which we are to be true, but
even what it is that we look for. Schiller wrote: 'Every
individual human being, one may say, carries within him,
potentially and prescriptively, an ideal man, the archetype
of a human being, and it is his life's task to be, through
all his changing manifestations, in harmony with the unchanging unity of this ideal.' The archetype of a human
being: is this then the own self? No doubt it is what
Matthew Arnold called the 'best self', but is it the own self?
Is it not the best self of mankind in general, rather than of
me in particular? And if it can be called mine in any sense,
if, because it is mankind's best self, it must therefore be my
best self, surely its being that exactly means it isn't (as Keats
called it) my sole self: I know that it coexists with another
self which is less good in the public moral way but which,
by very reason of its culpability, might be regarded as more
peculiarly mine. So Hawthorne thought: 'Be true! Be true!
Be true! Show freely to the world, if not your worst, yet
some trait by which the worst may be inferred.'

If sincerity is the avoidance of being false to any man
through being true to one's own self, we can see that this

state of personal existence is not to be attained without the most arduous effort. And yet at a certain point in history certain men and classes of men conceived that the making of this effort was of supreme importance in the moral life, and the value they attached to the enterprise of sincerity became a salient, perhaps a definitive, characteristic of Western culture for some four hundred years.

ii

A historical account of sincerity must take into its pur⁄view not only the birth and ascendancy of the concept but also its eventual decline, the sharp diminution of the autho⁄rity it once exercised. The word itself has lost most of its former high dignity. When we hear it, we are conscious of the anachronism which touches it with quaintness. If we speak it, we are likely to do so with either discomfort or irony. In its commonest employment it has sunk to the level of a mere intensive, in which capacity it has an effect that negates its literal intention—'I sincerely believe' has less weight than 'I believe'; in the subscription of a letter, 'Yours sincerely' means virtually the opposite of 'Yours'. To praise a work of literature by calling it sincere is now at best a way of saying that although it need be given no aesthetic or intellectual admiration, it was at least conceived in inno⁄cence of heart. When F. R. Leavis in all seriousness dis⁄tinguishes between those aspects of T. S. Eliot's work which are sincere and those which are not, we are inclined to note the distinction as an example of the engagingly archaic quality of Dr. Leavis's seriousness.

The devaluation of sincerity is bound up in an essential although paradoxical way with the mystique of the classic literature of our century, some of whose masters took the position that, in relation to their work and their audience, they were not persons or selves, they were artists, by which they meant that they were exactly not, in the phrase with which Wordsworth began his definition of the poet, men speaking to men. Their statements to this effect were famous in their time and are indelible in the memory of readers of a certain age. Eliot said that 'The progress of an artist is a continual self-sacrifice, a continual extinction of personality'. Joyce said that 'The personality of the artist . . . finally refines itself out of existence, impersonalizes itself, so to speak'. Gide—he of all people!—said that 'The aesthetic point of view is the only sound one to take in discussing my work'. Their achieved existence as artists precluded their being men speaking to men, from which it follows that the criterion of sincerity, the calculation of the degree of congruence between feeling and avowal, is not pertinent to the judgement of their work. The paradox to be discerned in the position begins, of course, in the extent to which the work of the great modern masters is preoccupied with personal concerns, with the self and with the difficulties of being true to it. If I may quote a characterization of the classic literature of the early century that I once had occasion to make, 'No literature has ever been so shockingly personal—it asks us if we are content with our marriages, with our professional lives, with our friends. . . . It asks us if we are content with ourselves, if we are saved or damned—more than with anything else, it is concerned with salvation.' And the paradox continues with the awareness, which we gain without any special effort, that this literature takes its licence to ask impermissible personal questions from its authors' having put the same questions to themselves. For all their intention of impersonality, they figure in our minds exactly as persons, as personalities, of a large exemplary kind, asking, each one of them, what his own self is and whether or not he is being true to it, drawing us to the emulation of their self-scrutiny. Their statements about the necessity of transcending or extirpating the personal self we take to be an expression of the fatigues which that self is fated to endure; or perhaps we under-stand them as a claim to shamanistic power: not I but the wind, the spirit, uttered these words.

The doctrine of the impersonality of the artist was loyally seconded by the criticism that grew up with the classic modern literature. In its dealings with personality this criti-cism played an elaborate, ambiguous, and arbitrary game. While seeking to make us ever more sensitive to the implica-tions of the poet's voice in its unique quality, including inevitably those implications that are personal before they are moral and social, it was at the same time very strict in its insistence that the poet is not a person at all, only a *persona*, and that to impute to him a personal existence is a breach of literary decorum.

This chaste view of literature doubtless had its corrective uses. But the day seems to have passed when the simple truth that criticism is not gossip requires to be enforced by precepts which forbid us to remark the resemblances between Stephen Dedalus and James Joyce or between Michel or Jérome and André Gide. We are no longer re-quired to regard as wholly fortuitous the fact that the hero of Proust's novel is named Marcel. Within the last two decades English and American poets have programmatic-ally scuttled the sacred doctrine of the *persona*, the belief that the poet does not, must not, present himself to us and figure in our consciousness as a person, as a man speaking to men, but must have an exclusively aesthetic existence. The aban-donment of this once crucial article of faith has been com-memorated by Donald Davie in an interesting essay. As Mr. Davie puts it, 'A poem in which the "I" stands immediately and unequivocally for the author' is at the present time held to be 'essentially and necessarily superior to a poem in which the "I" stands not for the author but for a *persona* of the author's'. This striking reversal of doctrine Mr. Davie speaks of as a return to the romanticist valuation of sincerity; the title he gives to his essay is: 'On Sincerity: From Wordsworth to Ginsberg.'

I do not wish to cut the matter too fine—the word 'sincerity' will serve well enough for what Mr. Davie has in mind. Yet I think we will come closer to comprehending the development he describes if we use some other word to denote it. The unmediated exhibition of the self, presumably with the intention of being true to it, which Mr. Davie remarks as characteristic of many contemporary poets, is not with final appropriateness to be called an effort of sincerity because it does not involve the reason that Polonius gives for being true to one's own self: that if one is, one cannot then be false to any man. This purpose no longer has its old urgency. Which is not to say that the moral temper of our time sets no store by the avoidance of falsehood to others, only that it does not figure as the defining purpose of being true to one's own self. If sincerity has lost its former status, if the word itself has for us a hollow sound and seems almost to negate its meaning, that is because it does not propose being true to one's own self as an end but only as a means. If one is true to one's own self for the purpose of avoiding falsehood to others, is one being truly true to one's own self? The moral end in view implies a public end in view, with all that this suggests of the esteem and fair repute that follow upon the correct fulfilment of a public role.

I did not deliberately choose that last word. It came readily—'naturally'—to hand. We nowadays say 'role' without taking thought of its original histrionic meaning: 'in my professional role', 'in my paternal, or maternal, role', even 'in my masculine, or feminine, role'. But the old

histrionic meaning is present whether or not we let ourselves be aware of it, and it brings with it the idea that
somewhere under all the roles there is Me, that poor old
ultimate actuality, who, when all the roles have been
played, would like to murmur 'Off, off, you lendings!' and
settle down with his own original actual self.

It is surely no accident that the idea of sincerity, of the
own self and the difficulty of knowing and showing it,
should have arisen to vex men's minds in the epoch that
saw the sudden efflorescence of the theatre.[1] A well-known
contemporary work of sociology bears the title, *The Presentation of Self in Everyday Life*—we can suppose that the
Hamlet of our day says: 'I have that within which passeth
presentation.' In this enterprise of presenting the self, of
putting ourselves on the social stage, sincerity itself plays a
curiously compromised part. Society requires of us that we
present ourselves as being sincere, and the most efficacious
way of satisfying this demand is to see to it that we really

---

[1] But see Eric Bentley's 'Theatre and Therapy', *New American Review*, viii
(1970), pp. 133–4. 'The idea that "all the world's a stage/And all the men and
women merely players", is not a clever improvisation casually tossed off by
Shakespeare's cynic Jaques, it is a commonplace of Western civilization. It is
a truth and was written on the wall of Shakespeare's theatre, the Globe, in
a language older than English: "*Totus mundus facit histrionem.*" To speak of life,
as many psychiatrists do, as role-playing is only to make a new phrase, not to
advance a new idea.' That the idea is an old one must certainly be granted—
see, for example, on page 86 of the present volume, Hans Jonas's comment
on the histrionic element in the Stoic morality. Yet, as I have suggested earlier,
there have been cultural epochs in which men did not think of themselves as
having a variety of selves or roles. Mr. Bentley goes on to assert both the in-
evitability and the positive value of role-playing. 'It is curious', he says, 'how
the phrase "play-acting" has come to be a slur; it implies insincerity. Yet the
commonplaces I have cited imply that one has no alternative to play-acting.
The choice is only between one role and another. And this is precisely the
positive side of the idea: that we do have a choice, that life does offer us alterna-
tives. . . .' The point is persuasively made but it doesn't, I think, silence the
insistent claims of the own self.

are sincere, that we actually are what we want our com⁄
munity to know we are. In short, we play the role of being
ourselves, we sincerely act the part of the sincere person,
with the result that a judgement may be passed upon our
sincerity that it is not authentic.

The word 'authenticity' comes so readily to the tongue
these days and in so many connections that it may very well
resist such efforts of definition as I shall later make, but I
think that for the present I can rely on its suggesting a more
strenuous moral experience than 'sincerity' does, a more
exigent conception of the self and of what being true to it
consists in, a wider reference to the universe and man's
place in it, and a less acceptant and genial view of the
social circumstances of life. At the behest of the criterion
of authenticity, much that was once thought to make up the
very fabric of culture has come to seem of little account,
mere fantasy or ritual, or downright falsification. Con⁄
versely, much that culture traditionally condemned and
sought to exclude is accorded a considerable moral autho⁄
rity by reason of the authenticity claimed for it, for example,
disorder, violence, unreason. The concept of authenticity
can deny art itself, yet at the same time it figures as the dark
source of art: so it did for Yeats, himself no mean role⁄
player and lover of *personae*, at a moment when all his per⁄
formances seemed to him of no account and he had to
discover how to devise new ones.

> Those masterful images because complete
> Grew in pure mind, but out of what began?
> A mound of refuse or the sweepings of a street,
> Old kettles, old bottles, and a broken can,
> Old iron, old bones, old rags, that raving slut
> Who keeps the till. Now that my ladder's gone,
> I must lie down where all the ladders start,
> In the foul rag⁄and⁄bone shop of the heart.

A very considerable originative power had once been claimed for sincerity, but nothing to match the marvellous generative force that our modern judgement assigns to authenticity, which implies the downward movement through all the cultural superstructures to some place where all movement ends, and begins. 'Look in thy heart and write', says Sir Philip Sidney's Muse to the poet—how all too blithe that old injunction sounds to our modern ears! There is no foul rag⁄and⁄bone shop in *that* heart. It is not the heart of darkness.

Still, before authenticity had come along to suggest the deficiencies of sincerity and to usurp its place in our esteem, sincerity stood high in the cultural firmament and had dominion over men's imagination of how they ought to be.

iii

The word itself enters the English language in the first third of the sixteenth century, considerably later than its appearance in French.[1] It derived from the Latin word *sincerus* and first meant exactly what the Latin word means in its literal use—clean, or sound, or pure. An old and merely fanciful etymology, *sine cera*, without wax, had in mind an object of virtu which was not patched up and passed off as sound, and serves to remind us that the word in its early use referred primarily not to persons but to things, both material and immaterial. One spoke of sincere wine, not in a metaphorical sense, in the modern fashion of describing the taste of a wine by attributing some moral

[1] The *O.E.D.* gives 1549 as the date of the earliest French use, but this is contradicted by Paul Robert's *Dictionnaire alphabétique et analogique de la langue française* (1960–4), which gives 1475 as the date for *sincère* and 1237 as the date for *sincérité*. The word does not appear in Frédéric Godefroy's *Dictionnaire de l'ancienne langue française et de tous ses dialectes du IXe au XVe siècles* (1892).

quality to it, but simply to mean that it had not been adulterated, or, as was once said, sophisticated. In the language of medicine urine might be sincere, and there was sincere fat and sincere gall. To speak of the sincere doctrine, or the sincere religion, or the sincere Gospel, was to say that it had not been tampered with, or falsified, or corrupted. Dr. Johnson in his Dictionary gives priority to the meaning of the word as applied to things rather than to persons. As used in the early sixteenth century in respect of persons, it is largely metaphorical—a man's life is sincere in the sense of being sound, or pure, or whole; or consistent in its virtuousness. But it soon came to mean the absence of dissimulation or feigning or pretence. Shakespeare uses the word only in this latter sense, with no apparent awareness of its ever having been used metaphorically.

The sixteenth century was preoccupied to an extreme degree with dissimulation, feigning, and pretence. Dante had assigned those whose 'deeds were not of the lion but of the fox' to the penultimate circle of the Inferno, but Machiavelli reversed the judgement, at least in public life, by urging upon the Prince the way of the fox. In doing so he captivated the literary mind of England in the Elizabethan age and became, as Wyndham Lewis put it, the master figure of its drama. But the fascination with the idea of the Machiavell cannot alone account for the extent to which that drama exploited the false presentation of the self. 'I am not what I am' could have been said not alone by Iago but by a multitude of Shakespeare's virtuous characters at some point in their careers. Hamlet has no sooner heard out the Ghost than he resolves to be what he is not, a madman. Rosalind is not a boy, Portia is not a doctor of law, Juliet is not a corpse, the Duke Vicentio is not a friar, Edgar is not Tom o' Bedlam, Hermione is neither dead nor a statue. Helena is not Diana, Mariana is not Isabella—

the credence the Elizabethan audience gave to the ancient 'bed-trick', in which a woman passes herself off as another during a night of love, suggests the extent of its commit-ment to the idea of impersonation.

But although innocent feigning has its own very great interest, it is dissimulation in the service of evil that most commands the moral attention. The word 'villain' as used in drama carries no necessary meaning of dissembling—it is possible for a villain not to compound his wickedness with deceit, to be overt in his intention of doing harm. Yet the fact that in the lists of dramatis personae in the First Folio Iago alone is denominated 'a villain' suggests that, in his typical existence, a villain is a dissembler, his evil nature apparent to the audience but concealed from those with whom he treads the boards.

And it is thus that the conception of the villain survived well into the Victorian era. A characteristic of the literary culture of the post-Victorian age was the discovery that villains were not, as the phrase went, 'true to life', and that to believe in the possibility of their existence was naïve. It became established doctrine that people were 'a mixture of good and bad' and that much of the bad could be accounted for by 'circumstances'. The diminished credibility of the villain, the opinion that he was appropriate only to the fantasy of melodrama, not to the truth of serious novels or plays, may in part be explained by the modern tendency to locate evil in social systems rather than in persons. But it is worth considering whether it might not also have come about because the dissembling which defined the villain became less appropriate to new social circumstances than it had been to preceding ones. Perhaps it should not be taken for granted that the villain was nothing but a con-vention of the stage which for a time was also adopted by the novel. There is ground for believing that the villain was once truer to life than he later became. We cannot establish by actual count that there were more villains in real life at one time than at another, but we can say that there was at one time better reason, more practical use, for villainous dissembling than at another. Tartuffe, Blifil, *la cousine* Bette, Mme Marneffe, Uriah Heep, Blandois, Becky Sharp—these wolves in sheep's clothing are not free fantasies, and it is a misapprehension to think of them as such. The possibility of their actual existence is underwritten by social fact.

It is a historical commonplace that, beginning in the sixteenth century, there was a decisive increase in the rate of social mobility, most especially in England but also in France. It became more and more possible for people to leave the class into which they were born. The middle class rose, not only in its old habitual way but unprecedentedly. Yet, striking as the new social mobility was compared with that of the past, from our present point of view it must seem to have been most inadequate to the social desires that had come into being. Tocqueville's principle of revolutions is here in point, that in the degree to which the gratification of social desires begins to be possible, impatience at the hindrances to gratification increases. And how effectual these hindrances were may be learned from any good English or French novel of the nineteenth century. Tocqueville pressed it upon the attention of the French that England had gained much in the way of political stability from the licence given to upward mobility by the commodious English idea of the 'gentleman'; yet we cannot fail to be aware of how limited that mobility was, how quick was the class of gentlemen to remark the social stigmata that made a man unfit for membership in it. A salient fact of French and English society up to a hundred years ago is the paucity of honourable professions which could serve the ambitious as avenues of social advancement. To a society thus restricted, the scheme, the plot, do not seem alien; the forging or destroying of wills is a natural form of economic enterprise. The system of social deference was still of a kind to encourage flattery as a means of personal ingratiation and advancement. The original social meaning of the word 'villain' bears decisively upon its later moral meaning. The opprobrious term referred to the man who stood lowest in the scale of feudal society; the villain of plays and novels is characteristically a person who seeks to rise above the station to which he was born. He is not what he is: this can be said of him both because by his intention he denies and violates his social identity and because he can achieve his unnatural purpose only by covert acts, by guile. In the nature of his case, he is a hypocrite, which is to say one who plays a part. It is to the point that Iago's resentment of his class situation and his wish to better it are conspicuous in his character.

The hypocrite-villain, the conscious dissembler, has become marginal, even alien, to the modern imagination of the moral life. The situation in which a person systematically misrepresents himself in order to practise upon the good faith of another does not readily command our interest, scarcely our credence. The deception we best understand and most willingly give our attention to is that which a person works upon himself. Iago's avowed purpose of base duplicity does not hold for us the fascination that nineteenth-century audiences found in it; our liveliest curiosity is likely to be directed to the moral condition of Othello, to what lies hidden under his superbness, to what in him is masked by the heroic *persona*. Similarly Tartuffe, who consciously and avowedly dissembles, engages us less than the protagonist of *Le Misanthrope*, who, Molière suggests, despite the programmatic completeness of his sincerity is not entirely what he is. 'My chief talent is to be frank and sincere', Alceste says. The whole energy of his being is directed towards perfecting the trait upon which he prides himself. '... *Dont son âme se pique*': it is the clue to the comic flaw. Every ridiculous person in the play has his point of pride; for Oronte it is his sonnets, for Clitandre his waist‑coats, for Acaste his noble blood, his wealth, and his infallible charm. Alceste's point of pride is his sincerity, his remorseless outspokenness on behalf of truth. The obsessiveness and obduracy of his sincerity amount to *hubris*, that state of being in which truth is obscured through the ascendancy of self‑regarding will over intelligence. It is to his will and not, as he persuades himself, to truth that Alceste gives his stern allegiance.

No laughter at human weakness was ever more charged with compunction and tenderness than that which Molière directs upon the self‑deception of Alceste's sincerity. Of this Rousseau would seem to have had no awareness when, in the *Lettre à M. d'Alembert sur les spectacles*, he framed his famous denunciation of *Le Misanthrope*. Not that Rousseau was not himself moved to compunction and tenderness in his attack—he spoke more in sorrow than in anger and chastised where he loved, for he adored Molière and, for all the severity of his strictures on the play, he especially ad‑mired *Le Misanthrope*. In it, we may suppose, he saw his own portrait drawn, and the root of his quarrel with Molière is that the radical moral absolutism of Alceste is not celebrated but questioned and teased. It was not the intention of Molière in his comedies, Rousseau says, to set up the model of a good man but rather that of a man of the world, a likeable man; he did not wish to correct vices but only what is ridiculous, 'and of all ridiculous characters the one which the world pardons least is the one who is ridicu‑lous because he is virtuous'. *Le Misanthrope*, Rousseau goes

on, was written 'to please corrupt minds'; it represents a
'false good' which is more dangerous than actual evil,
causing 'the practice and the principles of society to be
preferred to exact probity' and making 'wisdom consist in
a certain mean between vice and virtue'.

This is a reading of the play that everyone must make. It
consorts with the common view of the moral principle of
Molière's comedies, which is that right conduct is sensible
conduct, involving a large element of pragmatic accommodation to society's deficiencies and contradictions. But
with this reading must go another, which takes account of
the perception that Alceste's feelings and opinions are
Molière's own, that the bland good sense of Alceste's loyal
friend Philinte does not really have the last word, that
Célimène is not only all that George Meredith says she is
in the way of charm and vitality but also a whited sepulchre
and as such an allegory of society itself.

For our present purpose of identifying a chief circumstance with which the origin and rise of sincerity is bound
up, it does not matter which of the two readings best re-
commends itself, since one as decisively as the other places
the concept of *society* at the centre of the play. What occupies and tortures the mind of Alceste is not that first one
and then another of the members of his immediate circle,
and then still another and at last almost all of them, out of
vanity or for material advantage, make avowals which are
not in accord with what they feel or believe, but rather that
the life of man in a developed community must inevitably
be a corruption of truth. When in the end Alceste vows
himself to solitude, it is not out of mere personal dis-
appointment in the entrancing Célimène but out of
disgust with society, an entity whose nature is not to be
exactly defined by the nature of the individuals who
constitute it.

In his book *Culture and Society* Raymond Williams examines certain words, now of capital importance in our speech, which first came into use in their present meaning in the last decades of the eighteenth century and in the first half of the nineteenth: 'industry', 'democracy', 'class', 'art', and 'culture'. These words make our way of thinking about society. And although Mr. Williams does not say so, 'society' itself is another such word. The provenance of its present meaning is older than that of the others, but it too came into use at a particular time—in the sixteenth century —and we can observe not only its ever-increasing currency but also its ever-widening range of connotation. Society is a concept that is readily hypostatized—the things that are said about it suggest that it has a life of its own and its own laws. An aggregate of individual human beings, society is yet something other than this, something other than human, and its being conceived in this way, as having indeed a life of its own but not a human life, gives rise to the human desire to bring it into accord with humanity. Society is a kind of entity different from a kingdom or realm; and even 'commonwealth', as Hobbes uses that word, seems archaic to denote what he has in mind.

Historians of European culture are in substantial agree-ment that, in the late sixteenth and early seventeenth cen-turies, something like a mutation in human nature took place. Frances Yates speaks of 'the inner deep-seated changes in the psyche during the early seventeenth century', which she calls 'the vital period for the emergence of modern European and American man'. The changes were most dramatically marked in England, and Zevedei Barbu describes what he calls 'the formation of a new type of personality, which embodies the main traits of English national character throughout the modern era'. Paul Delany in his study of the sudden efflorescence of autobiography in the period remarks 'some deep change in the British habits of thought' that must account for the development of the new genre. The unfolding public events with which the psychological changes are connected—equally, we note, as cause and as effect—are the dissolution of the feudal order and the diminished authority of the Church. One way of giving a synopsis of the whole complex psycho-historical occurrence is to say that the idea of society, much as we now conceive it, had come into being.

The decline of feudalism issued in the unprecedented social mobility I have touched on, with, expectably enough, an ever-increasing urbanization of the population. In 1550 London was a city of some 60,000 souls; within a hundred years the number had increased nearly six times to about 350,000. This is a condition of life that literature has chiefly deplored and for many generations the educated bour-geoisie has characteristically shuddered away from the moral and spiritual effects of the circumstance from which it derives its being and its name. Its vision of the good life, so far as it has been enlightened and polemical, has been largely shaped by the imagination of the old rural existence. For Karl Marx, however, the city was to be praised for at least one thing, the escape it offers from what he called 'the idiocy of village life'. He no doubt had in mind the primi-tive meaning of the word 'idiot', which is not a mentally deficient person, nor yet an uncouth and ignorant person, but a private person, one 'who does not hold public office': a person who is not a participant in society as Marx under-stood it. For Marx the working out of the historical process, and therefore the essential life of man, could take place only in cities, where the classes confront each other, where men in the mass demonstrate the nature and destiny of mankind. In the swarming of men in cities—in *Schwärmerei*, as Carlyle called it, meaning contemptuously to invoke both the physical and the emotional meaning of the German word—society forced itself upon the very senses: before it was ever an idea to be thought about, it was a thing to be seen and heard.[1]

Society was seen and heard, and thought about, by men who had liberated themselves from the sanctions of the corporate Church. To the Calvinist divines of England, predications about society and the ways in which it was to be shaped and controlled came as readily as predications about divinity and the divine governance of the world. Michael Walzer makes the suggestion that these Calvinist leaders are 'the first instance of "advanced" intellectuals in a traditional society' and gives to his book about them, *The Revolution of the Saints*, the descriptive subtitle, *A Study in the Origins of Radical Politics*—which is to say, a politics in which partisanship is based not upon discrete practical issues but upon a formulated conception of what society is and a prophecy of what it is to be. The divines were intellectuals in their reliance upon the Word and in their resolution to speak it out plain for all to hear. Like Molière's Alceste, they regarded society as fallen into corruption

[1] Peter Laslett emphasizes 'the minute scale of life, the small size of human groups before the coming of industry'. See *The World We Have Lost: England Before the Industrial Age* (Scribner's, New York; Methuen, London, 1965), p. 51; also pp. 9–11 and 74. The church service, Mr. Laslett says, was the occasion most likely to bring people together in groups larger than a household. He mentions also the assizes of the county towns, the quarter sessions of the county justices, meetings of craft associations, assemblies of the clergy and of Nonconformist ministers, market days, the universities, the army, and Parliament. His point is that all these groups were small by comparison with the groups that are characteristic of modern mass society, which did not begin to come into being until the middle and late eighteenth century when factories were established. But it should be remarked that by the end of the sixteenth century the theatres were bringing people together in quite considerable numbers —the spectators at a performance at the Globe (1598) and at the Fortune (1600) commonly numbered a thousand, and both theatres are thought to have had capacities of more than two thousand.

through false avowal; like him, the talent on which they most prided themselves was that of being sincere, telling the offensive truth to those who had no wish to hear it.

Plain speaking became the order of the day. How new a thing this was and how worthy to be remarked in its heady novelty is suggested by an episode in the fourth book of Castiglione's *Courtier*. By this point in the dialogues the character of the ideal courtier, the perfect man, has been fully drawn. Everything that he should be by reason of his noble birth and his study and labour to be beautiful has been stipulated. And now, after so much has been agreed upon, one of the company, Signor Ottaviano, raises the disquieting question of whether the whole enterprise of making the perfect self, as one might make a work of art, can after all be taken seriously. Does the achieved grace and charm, Ottaviano asks, constitute anything but a frivolity and a vanity, even an unmanliness? The effort to achieve this grace and charm is to be praised, he says, only if it serves some good and serious purpose. But then Ottaviano himself discovers that there is indeed such a purpose. The perfect courtier will be so attractive to his Prince that he can depend on not falling out of favour when he speaks plain, or nearly plain, telling the Prince—'in a gentle manner'— in what respects his conduct of affairs is not what it should be. In Italy in 1518 one could speak plain to sovereign power only if one possessed a trained perfection of grace and charm. In England a century later the only requirement for speaking plain was a man's conviction that he had the Word to speak. I would not press the point, but it does seem to be of significance in the developing political culture of the time that Shakespeare, in what nowadays is often said to be his greatest play, should set so much store by plain speaking and ring so many changes on the theme, what with Cordelia, who by nature is the perfection of courtesy, and Kent, whose style is the negation of Castiglione's discipline of courtliness, and the Fool, and Cornwall's astonishing peasant: a blessed hierarchy of English plain speakers.

In England the nature of the sovereign had, of course, changed. The Calvinist divines, when they spoke the plain word to the sovereign prince, derived their moral and intellectual authority from their relation to the divine Word, but also from their awareness of the sovereign many, the people, to whom their discourses on society were addressed, who were ready to receive the Word plainspoken. There was an external as well as an internal sanction for their reliance on the Word.

The internal sanction could never, it is true, be proved, but its probability might be enforced. If one spoke publicly on great matters as an individual, one's only authority was the truth of one's experience and the intensity of one's conviction of enlightenment—these, and the accent of sincerity, clearly identifiable as such. It therefore cannot surprise us that at this point in time autobiography should have taken its rise in England. The genre, as Delany observes, is by no means exclusively Protestant, but it is predominantly so. Its earliest examples are not elaborate; chiefly they are sparse records of the events of religious experience. But the form continues to press towards a more searching scrutiny of the inner life, its purpose being to enforce upon the reader the conclusion that the writer cannot in any respect be false to any man because he has been true to himself, as he was and is. Rousseau's *Confessions* exists, of course, in a different dimension of achievement from these first English autobiographies, but it is continuous with them. The *Confessions* was not a gratuitous undertaking. It was the painstaking demonstration of the author's authority to speak

plain, to bring into question every aspect of society. Anyone who responds to Rousseau's ideas in a positive way
must wonder whether they would have made an equal
effect upon him if they had not been backed by the *Confessions*. The person who is depicted in that great work may
repel us; but the author of the *Discourses* has the more
power over us because he is the subject of the *Confessions*.
He is the man; he suffered; he was there.

The impulse to write autobiography may be taken as
virtually definitive of the psychological changes to which
the historians point. Which is to say—although one rather
dreads saying it, so often has it been said before, so firmly
is it established in our minds as the first psycho-historical
concept we ever learned—that the new kind of personality
which emerges (the verb is tediously constant in the context) is what we call an 'individual': at a certain point in
history men became individuals.

Taken in isolation, the statement is absurd. How was a
man different from an individual? A person born before
a certain date, a man—had he not eyes? had he not hands,
organs, dimensions, senses, affections, passions? If you
pricked him, he bled and if you tickled him, he laughed.
But certain things he did not have or do until he became
an individual. He did not have an awareness of what one
historian, Georges Gusdorf, calls internal space. He did
not, as Delany puts it, imagine himself in more than one
role, standing outside or above his own personality; he did
not suppose that he might be an object of interest to his
fellow man not for the reason that he had achieved something notable or been witness to great events but simply
because as an individual he was of consequence. It is when
he becomes an individual that a man lives more and more in
private rooms; whether the privacy makes the individuality
or the individuality requires the privacy the historians do

not say.[1] The individual looks into mirrors, larger and much brighter than those that were formerly held up to magistrates. The French psychoanalyst Jacques Lacan be-lieves that the development of the '*Je*' was advanced by the manufacture of mirrors: again it cannot be decided whether man's belief that he is a '*Je*' is the result of the Venetian craftsmen's having learned how to make plate-glass or whether the demand for looking-glasses stimulated this technological success. If he is an artist the individual is likely to paint self-portraits; if he is Rembrandt, he paints some threescore of them. And he begins to use the word 'self' not as a mere reflexive or intensive, but as an autono-mous noun referring, the *O.E.D.* tells us, to 'that . . . in a person [which] is really and intrinsically *he* (in contra-distinction to what is adventitious)', as that which he must cherish for its own sake and show to the world for the sake of good faith. The subject of an autobiography is just such a self, bent on revealing himself in all his truth, bent, that is to say, on demonstrating his sincerity. His conception of his private and uniquely interesting individuality, together with his impulse to reveal his self, to demonstrate that in it which is to be admired and trusted, are, we may believe, his response to the newly available sense of an audience, of that public which society created.

[1] See Christopher Hill, *The Century of Revolution: 1603–1741* (Nelson, London; Norton, New York, 1961), p. 253: 'All roads in our period have led to individualism. More rooms in better-off peasant houses, use of glass in windows (common for copyholders and ordinary poor people only since the Civil War, Aubrey says); use of coal in grates, replacement of benches by chairs—all this made possible greater comfort and privacy for at least the upper half of the population. Privacy contributed to the introspection and soul-searching of radical Puritanism, to the keeping of diaries and spiritual journals. . . .' Mr. Hill is referring to the period 1660–80, after the defeat of Puritanism.

II · THE HONEST SOUL AND THE DISINTEGRATED CON-SCIOUSNESS

i

OUR INVESTIGATION OF SINCERITY HAS NO sooner begun than it has led to public and even to political considerations. This, if it is surprising at all, cannot be more than momentarily so. Doubtless, when we think about sincerity, we first conceive of it as a quality of the personal and private life, as bearing upon the individual's relation to himself and to others as individuals. Yet the intense concern with sincerity which came to characterize certain European national cultures at the beginning of the modern epoch would seem to have developed in connection with a great public event, the extreme revision of traditional modes of communal organization which gave rise to the entity that now figures in men's minds under the name of society. A salient trait of society, I have suggested, and what differentiates it from the realm or the kingdom and even from the commonwealth, is that it is available to critical examination by individual persons, especially by those who make it their business to scrutinize the polity, the class of men we now call intellectuals. The purpose of their examination is not understanding alone but understanding as it may lead to action: the idea of society includes the assumption that a given society can be changed if the judgement passed upon it is adverse. In the framing of such judgements the ideal of sincerity is of substantial

importance. It is adduced as a criterion in three considera'
tions: (1) Of the sincerity of the person making the judge'
ment. This must be beyond question and fully manifest.
(2) Of the degree of correspondence between the principles
avowed by a society and its actual conduct. (3) Of the
extent to which a society fosters, or corrupts, the sincerity
of its citizens.

The last of these considerations is the subject of a work
which must always have a special place in the develop'
ment of the ideal of sincerity, Diderot's great dialogue with
the scapegrace nephew of the composer Rameau. The date
of the composition of *Le Neveu de Rameau* is uncertain; it
was written some time between 1761 and 1774 and, for
reasons of discretion, was not published in its author's life'
time. Included among the books and manuscripts which
were purchased from Diderot by his patron Catherine the
Great, it was clandestinely copied, smuggled out of Russia,
and brought to Germany in 1803. Its subsequent career is
legendary and sums up the intellectual life of Europe for
a century. Schiller, when it was shown to him, recognized
its genius with rapture and rushed the manuscript to
Goethe, upon whom it burst, as he said, like a bombshell.
Such, indeed, was Goethe's enthusiasm for the dialogue
that he at once engaged to translate it. In order to annotate
the text he undertook a headlong reading of the French
literature of the eighteenth century, as a result of which he
recanted the famous adverse judgement he had made upon
the French mind in his student days at Strasbourg. Goethe's
translation, whose progress was Schiller's chief concern in
the last months of his life, was published in 1805. This was
the version read by Hegel, who cited the dialogue in
Phänomenologie des Geistes, enshrining it as a work of excep'
tional significance, the paradigm of the modern cultural
and spiritual situation. Part of Hegel's comment, which I

shall presently touch on, is quoted by Karl Marx in a letter to Engels in 1869 in which he says that, having just discovered that he owned two copies of *Rameau's Nephew*, he is sending one to his friend in Manchester for the 'fresh pleasure' this 'unique masterpiece' will give him. Freud read the dialogue with an admiration which was doubtless the more intense because its bestremembered passage, which he quoted on three occasions, formulates his Oedipal theory in unabashed simplicity: 'If your little savage [that is to say, any boy] were left to himself and to his native blindness, he would in time join the infant's reasoning to the grown man's passions—he would strangle his father and sleep with his mother.'

It is scarcely possible to describe the protagonist of the dialogue in a way that will be both summary and accurate. The significance of his character lies, of course, exactly in its contradictions. Because the younger Rameau breaks the taboos of respectable reticence and, at least on the occasion of his conversation with Diderot in the Café de la Régence, discloses all his desires, we are tempted to think that he is meant to represent the Freudian id, that he is a creature of 'drives', lustful, greedy, wholly obedient, as Freud says the id is, to the 'inexorable pleasureprinciple'. And this way of thinking about the Nephew seems the more permissible because of the virtuousness which marks his interlocutor; the Diderot of the dialogue is the avowed defender of rational morality. But in point of fact Rameau's behaviour is not iddirected. It is almost wholly under the control of the ego. His ruling concern is with selfpreservation, which, Freud tells us, is the ego's chief task. Out of this concern he is preoccupied, we might say obsessed, with society and with the desire for place and power in society. Above everything else, he longs for artistic success. In part he wants this for disinterested reasons, in part for the adulation and affluence it will bring. He is tortured by envy of his famous uncle, and bitter at having to live in his shadow.[1] His own talents are by no means negligible. His taste in music is exigent and censorious. His command of the musical reper-tory is prodigious, and by extravagant effort he has, as he puts it, subdued his fingers to do his will on the keyboard and strings. But despite his native abilities and the cruel self-discipline to which he has subjected himself, he must endure the peculiar bitterness of modern man, the know-ledge that he is not a genius. And although he is com-mitted to the purposes of the ego, which his superior intelligence might well allow him to achieve, he hardly manages to maintain himself. Reduced to a bare subsist-ence as a parasite at the tables of the rich, he directs all his ingenuity towards perfecting the devices of systematic flattery, yet he cannot succeed even in this miserable mode of life. His thwarted passion for what society has to offer goes along with a scornful nihilism which overwhelms every prudential consideration; he is the victim of an irresis-tible impulse to offend those with whom he seeks to ingratiate himself. And stronger than his desire for respect is his appetite for demonstrative self-abasement; his ego, betraying its proper function, turns on itself and finds ex-pression in a compulsive buffoonery, at once inviting shame and achieving shamelessness in a fashion that Dostoevsky was to make familiar. 'The fellow', Diderot says, 'is a compound of elevation and abjectness, of good sense and lunacy. . . . He has no greater opposite than himself.'

The characterization goes further: 'What a chimera . . . What a novelty, what a monster, what a chaos, what a contradiction, what a prodigy. Judge of all things,

---

[1] He still does, poor man—the Penguin translation of *Rameau's Nephew* displays on its cover a reproduction of Louis Carrogis Carmontelle's portrait of the great Rameau.

imbecile earthworm; depository of truth, sink of uncertainty
and error; glory and scum of the universe.' The words, of
course, are not Diderot's but Pascal's. Diderot's dialogue
continues and further particularizes Pascal's sense of the
human contradiction, of man as the opposite of himself.

The French Marxist critic Lucien Goldmann speaks of
Pascal as 'the first modern man'. By this he means that
Pascal anticipated the ideas of the German thinkers who
followed Kant, in particular Goethe, Hegel, and Marx.
One may the more readily suppose this to be true because
of the affinity the three men felt with Diderot—if it is
Diderot rather than Pascal himself whom Hegel chose to
exemplify the modern anthropology, one reason is that in
Rameau's Nephew, even more decisively than in the *Pensées*
of Pascal, society is understood to be the field on which
man runs his spiritual course. To be sure, nothing so much
confirms our awareness of the developing authority of the
concept of society as the extent to which it figures explicitly
in Pascal's representation of the difficulties of the religious
life. For Pascal, however, man's existence in society is but
the manifestation of his cosmic alienation, whereas for
Diderot the silence of the infinite spaces is not frightening;
it is not even heard. For Diderot society is all in all, the
root and ground of alienation. It is social man who is
alienated man.

In the great dialogue the alienation is very literal. It
begins with the name of the protagonist, who, the nature of
society being what it is, does not possess himself, is not his
own man—he is not Rameau but Rameau's nephew. 'This
nephew of Rameau's', the *Oxford Companion to French
Literature* is at pains to assure us, 'was a real person', but
the *Companion*, following Diderot himself, does not con-
descend to tell us his Christian name, which in point of
fact was Jean-François. The theory of society advanced by

the Nephew rests on his recognition of the systematic separa-
tion of the individual from his actual self. The social being,
he tells us, is a mere histrionic representation—every man
takes one or another 'position' as the choreography of
society directs. With the mimetic skill which is the essence
of his being, the Nephew demonstrates how he performs
the dance upon which his survival depends. 'Thereupon he
begins to smile, to ape a man admiring, a man imploring,
a man complying. His right foot forward, the left foot be-
hind, his back arched, head erect, his glance riveted as if
on someone's face, openmouthed, his arms are stretched
out toward some object. He waits for a command, receives
it, flies like an arrow, returns. The order has been carried
out; he is giving his report. He is all attention, nothing
escapes him. He picks up what is dropped, places pillow
or stool under feet, holds a salver, brings a chair, opens a
door, shuts a window, draws curtains, keeps his eye on
master and mistress. He is motionless, arms at his sides,
legs parallel; he listens and tries to read faces. Then he says,
"There you have my pantomime; it's about the same as the
flatterer's, the courtier's, the footman's, and the beggar's." '
The demonstration concluded, it is agreed between Diderot
and the Nephew, between the *Moi* and the *Lui* of the dialogue, that everyone in society, without exception, acts a
part, takes a 'position', does his dance, even the King himself, 'who takes a position before his mistress and God: he
dances his pantomime steps'.

No one is likely to read *Rameau's Nephew* without a ready
awareness of its ambiguity. In its first intention, which is
the one I have emphasized, the dialogue passes a direct and
comprehensively adverse moral judgement upon society. It
lays bare the principle of insincerity upon which society is
based and demonstrates the loss of personal integrity and
dignity that the impersonations of social existence entail.

But this is scarcely new; it had been the theme of the French moralists for more than a century, and even if we grant, as we readily do, that Diderot puts the moral case against society with unique dramatic force, this cannot of itself account for the charmed sense of discovery that the dialogue gave to so many great minds of the nineteenth century and still gives to lesser minds of a later day. The entrancing power of *Rameau's Nephew* is rather to be explained by its second intention, which is to suggest that moral judgement is not ultimate, that man's nature and destiny are not wholly comprehended within the narrow space between virtue and vice. From this comes the sensation of enlarge‑ ment, of delighted liberation, that the dialogue affords. Whatever is to be said in condemnation of the self‑seeking duplicity of society, of the great financiers, their wives and their little actresses and singers, and of the courtiers, and of the King himself, one person, the Nephew, transcends the moral categories and the judgement they dictate. Diderot the deuteragonist is at pains to treat him with discriminating condescension and to rebuke him for a deficiency of moral commitment, but we know that Diderot the author of the dialogue gives us full licence to take the Nephew to our hearts and minds, where he figures not only as an actual person but also as an aspect of humanity itself, as the liberty that we wish to believe is inherent in the human spirit, in its energy of effort, expectation, and desire, in its consciousness of itself and its limitless contradictions. The climax of the dialogue and, we might say, of its protagon‑ ist's existence, is Rameau's disquisition on the superiority of the new forms of opera to the old. The episode issues in his most elaborate mimetic display, for he proceeds to *be* opera, to impersonate the whole art—this musical Proteus, or perhaps he is to be called Panurge, sounds all the instru‑ ments, enacts all the roles, portraying all the emotions in all

voices and all modes. The astonishing performance proposes the idea which Nietzsche was to articulate a century
later, that man's true metaphysical destiny expresses itself
not in morality but in art.

Yet if the second intention of *Rameau's Nephew* is what
chiefly engages us and constitutes the genius of the work,
our particular pleasure in it must not lead us to slight the
first intention. The moral judgement which the dialogue
makes upon man in society is not finally rejected but coexists with its contradiction, and upon its validity and
weight depends the force of the idea that the moral categories may be transcended. And it is the Nephew himself
who invokes the moral categories at the same time that he
negates them—the moral judgement is grounded upon the
cogency of Rameau's observation of social behaviour and
the shamelessness with which he exhibits his own shame.

ii

When Hegel in the *Phenomenology of Mind* makes his
momentous comment on *Rameau's Nephew*, he follows and
carries to its extremity the line of the dialogue's second
intention. He acknowledges no debt to Diderot for the idea
that the nature and destiny of man are not ultimately to be
described in moral terms. Indeed, he seems to have per-
suaded himself that the dialogue is committed exclusively
to its moral first intention and he faults it for this limitation.
In the single section of the *Phenomenology* we shall have in
view,[1] Hegel holds moral judgement to be nothing but
retrograde, standing in the way of a true conception of the
human spirit. There is no trait whatever in the character of

[1] Pp. 509-48 of J. B. Baillie's translation (rev. 2nd ed., London, 1949;
New York, 1967).

the Nephew which he permits to be blamed or deplored. What any reader naturally understands as a deficiency in Rameau, to be forgiven or 'accepted', Hegel takes to be a positive attribute and of the highest significance, nothing less than a necessary condition of the development of Spirit, of *Geist*, that is to say, of mind in its defining act, which is to be aware of itself. Goethe's translation of the dialogue was published while the *Phenomenology* was in the course of composition; the Nephew, who is referred to in Goethe's text as a 'self-estranged spirit', was co-opted by Hegel to serve as the presiding genius of the section of his work called 'Spirit in Self-Estrangement'. Hegel represents the Nephew as the exemplary figure of the modern phase of developing Spirit and welcomes his advent with hiero-phantic glee.[1]

The difficulty of the *Phenomenology* is proverbial and this is not the occasion, nor have I the presumption, to attempt to recapitulate the whole complex process of self-estrange-ment as Hegel describes it. But there may be discerned through the great maze a path which the uninitiated can follow with at least a little confidence. Its direction is marked out by a vocabulary different from that which characterizes the work as a whole—amid the idiosyncratic distractions of Hegel's terminology we find certain words that are comforting in their familiarity, such words as 'nobility', 'baseness', 'service', 'heroism', 'flattery', and a combination of the last two in a strange and possibly witty phrase, 'the heroism of flattery'. We perceive that with these words Hegel is describing a historical development which is, to be sure, abstract and paradigmatic but also concrete and actual. So far as it is concrete and actual, it has par-

---

[1] At no point in his comment on the dialogue does Hegel mention either its title or the names of its author and its protagonist. In Baillie's translation the work to which Hegel refers is identified in an editorial footnote.

ticular reference to the social and cultural development of the Renaissance and the Enlightenment, and, as we cannot fail to perceive, of our own time.

The historical process that Hegel undertakes to expound is the self-realization of Spirit through the changing relation of the individual to the external power of society in two of its aspects, the political power of the state and the power of wealth. In an initial stage of the process that is being described the individual consciousness is said to be in a wholly harmonious relation to the external power of society, to the point of being identified with it. In this relation the individual consciousness renders what Hegel calls 'obedient service' to the external power and feels for it an 'inner reverence'. Its service is not only obedient but also silent and unreasoned, taken for granted; Hegel calls this 'the heroism of dumb service'. This entire and inarticulate accord of the individual consciousness with the external power of society is said to have the attribute of 'nobility'.

But the harmonious relation of the individual consciousness to the state power and to wealth is not destined to endure. It is the nature of Spirit, Hegel tells us, to seek 'existence on its own account'—that is, to free itself from limiting conditions, to press towards autonomy. In rendering 'obedient service' to and in feeling 'inner reverence' for anything except itself it consents to the denial of its own nature. If it is to fulfil its natural destiny of self-realization, it must bring to an end its accord with the external power of society. And in terminating this 'noble' relation the individual consciousness moves towards a relation with external power which Hegel calls 'base'.

The change is not immediate. Between the noble relation of the individual consciousness to state power and to wealth and the developing base relation there stands what Hegel speaks of as a 'mediating term'. In this transitional stage the 'heroism of dumb service' modifies itself to be come a heroism which is not dumb but articulate, what Hegel calls the 'heroism of flattery'. The individual, that is to say, becomes conscious of his relation to the external power of society; he becomes conscious of having made the choice to maintain the relationship and of the prudential reasons which induced him to make it—the 'flattery' is, in effect, the rationale of his choice which the individual formulates in terms of the virtues of the external power, presumably a personal monarch. We might suppose that Hegel had in mind the relation of the court aristocracy to Louis XIV. Consciousness and choice, it is clear, imply a commitment to, rather than an identification with, the external power of society.

From this modification of the 'noble' relation to the external power the individual proceeds to the 'baseness' of being actually antagonistic to the external power. What was once served and reverenced now comes to be regarded with resentment and bitterness. Hegel's description of the new attitude is explicit: 'It [that is, the individual con sciousness] looks upon the authoritative power of the state as a chain, as something suppressing its separate autono mous existence, and hence hates the ruler, obeys only with secret malice and stands ever ready to burst out in rebellion.' And the relation of the individual self to wealth is even baser, if only because of the ambivalence which marks it— the self loves wealth but at the same time despises it; through wealth the self 'attains to the enjoyment of its own inde pendent existence', but it finds wealth discordant with the nature of Spirit, for it is of the nature of Spirit to be per manent, whereas enjoyment is evanescent.

The process thus described makes an unhappy state of affairs but not, as Hegel judges it, by any means a deplor able one. He intends us to understand that the movement from 'nobility' to 'baseness' is not a devolution but a development. So far from deploring 'baseness', Hegel cele‑brates it. And he further confounds our understanding by saying that 'baseness' leads to and therefore *is* 'nobility'. What is the purpose of this high‑handed inversion of common meanings?

An answer might begin with the observation that the words 'noble' and 'base', although they have been assimi‑lated to moral judgement, did not originally express con‑cepts of moral law, of a prescriptive and prohibitory code which is taken to be of general, commanding, and even supernal authority and in which a chief criterion of a person's rightdoing and wrongdoing is the effect of his conduct upon other persons. The words were applied, rather, to the ideal of personal existence of a ruling class at a certain time—its ethos, in that sense of the word which conveys the idea not of abstractly *right* conduct but of a characteristic manner or style of *approved* conduct. What is in accord with this ethos is noble; what falls short of it or derogates from it is base. The noble self is not shaped by its beneficent intentions towards others; its intention is wholly towards itself, and such moral virtue as may be attributed to it follows incidentally from its expressing the privilege and function of its social status in mien and de‑portment. We might observe that the traits once thought appropriate to the military life are definitive in the forma‑tion of the noble self. It stands before the world boldly defined, its purposes clearly conceived and openly avowed. In its consciousness there is no division, it is at one with itself. The base self similarly expresses a social condition, in the first instance by its characteristic mien and deportment, as these are presumed or required to be, and ultimately by the way in which it carries out those of its purposes that are self‑serving beyond the limits deemed appropriate to its social status. These purposes can be realized only by covert means and are therefore shameful. Between the intentions of the base self and its avowals there is no congruence. But the base self, exactly because it is not under the control of the noble ethos, has won at least a degree of autonomy and has thereby fulfilled the nature of Spirit. In refusing its obedient service to the state power and to wealth it has lost its wholeness; its selfhood is 'disintegrated'; the self is 'alienated' from itself. But because it has detached itself from imposed conditions, Hegel says that it has made a step in progress. He puts it that the existence of the self 'on its own account is, strictly speaking, the loss of itself'. The statement can also be made the other way round: 'Aliena/tion of self is really self-preservation.'

It is in the light of this phenomenological history of Spirit that Hegel hands down his uncompromising judge/ment as between the *Moi* and the *Lui* of Diderot's dialogue. His reading of the work is not that of the common reader, who, while taking all due account of the differences of character and opinion of the two speakers, will also remark the considerable extent of their agreement and will not understand the dialogue to be an unreconcilable litigation between them. But Hegel does, and he rules wholly in favour of Rameau, wholly against Diderot.

In referring to Diderot-*Moi* Hegel speaks of him as the 'honest soul' or the 'honest consciousness'. This might seem a praiseworthy kind of soul, a good kind of conscious/ness, to be; and we the more readily suppose so because of our admiration for the actual Diderot. But Hegel does not intend praise; the epithet 'honest' is used in its old con/descending sense, implying a limitation both of mind and of power. The 'honesty' of Diderot-*Moi*, which evokes Hegel's impatient scorn, consists in his wholeness of self, in the directness and consistency of his relation to things, and in his submission to a traditional morality. Diderot-*Moi* does not exemplify the urge of Spirit to escape from the conditions which circumscribe it and to enter into an existence which will be determined by itself alone.

It would make things easier if we could say that Hegel condemns Diderot-*Moi* because he is 'noble'. And perhaps we are licensed to say just that, despite all the considerations which make the use of the word seem inappropriate. It is true that the kind of self, or soul, or consciousness that Diderot-*Moi* represents, far from having affinity with a traditional noble class, consorts with the vision of life held by a class characterized exactly by its opposition to the ethos of a nobility. The actual Diderot, who has a pretty clear connection with Diderot-*Moi*, was a comfortable, clever, sensitive, voluble man in woollen stockings who laboured long years at his great *Encyclopédie*, an enterprise designed to bring to an end the power of the class from which the ideal of the noble derives. Yet in the face of the apparent contradiction it is still possible to say that the 'honesty' of Diderot's soul is of a kind that Hegel associates with the noble vision of life. It is a vision given supreme expression in the late plays of Shakespeare, the ones we call romances.

In adducing these plays I mean to suggest something of the simplest sort: only that the norm of life which they propose is one of order, peace, honour, and beauty, these qualities being realized in, and dependent upon, certain material conditions. The hope that animates this normative vision of the plays is the almost shockingly elementary one which Ferdinand utters in *The Tempest*—the hope of 'quiet days, fair issue, and long life'. It is reiterated by Juno in Prospero's pageant: 'Honour, riches, marriage blessing, / Long continuance and increasing.' It has to do with good harvests and full barns and the qualities of affluent decorum that Ben Jonson celebrated in Penshurst and Marvell in Appleton House, that Yeats prayed for in his daughter's domestic arrangements.

The mention of Yeats brings to mind the social event that occupied and distressed his thought through all his career, the defeat inflicted upon the old noble ethos by plebeian democracy. That defeat was in train and understood by many to be a foregone conclusion long before Yeats ever began to fret over it, and of its decisiveness there can be no question. Yet it is plain that the old ethos, though vanquished, did not suddenly lose every vestige of its power, but continued to exercise a considerable authority through the nineteenth century and even into the early twentieth century, perhaps especially in the life of England but of other nations as well. The novels read by the educated middle classes of England and France had as their heroes young men who believed in a condition of being that went by the name of happiness. This condition was to be achieved by attaining certain worldly objectives which were identical with the elements of the good life prescribed in Shakespeare's romances, including marriage with young women who were to be as much as possible like Perdita and Miranda. The self that imagined these objectives and sought to attain them was—or at least began by being—the kind of self that Hegel calls the 'honest soul' or the 'honest consciousness'.

The best of the novelists of the nineteenth century and of the beginning of our own epoch were anything but confident that the old vision of the noble life could be realized. But in the degree to which Balzac, Stendhal, Dickens, Trollope, Flaubert, and Henry James were aware of the probability of its defeat in actuality, they cherished and celebrated the lovely dream. The young James Joyce gave it a name, one that suggests both its anachronism and its allure—he spoke of his desire to enter 'the fair courts of life'. In that phrase, nostalgically recalling the vanished noble dispensation, he expressed all that the world in the time of his youth might still be fancied to offer in the way of order, peace, honour, and beauty. The credence that could formerly be given to material and social establishment and the happiness which followed from it was the very ground of the moral life as the novelists once represented it—the moral career began with the desire to enter the fair courts of life; how one con⁄ducted oneself in that enterprise was what morality was about.

In the literature of our own day, it need scarcely be said, the visionary norm of order, peace, honour, and beauty has no place. Conceivably its presence is to be discerned in its absence: the bitter contemptuous rejection of it that marks contemporary literature might perhaps be thought of as the expression of despair over the impossibility of realizing the vision. But also the rejection is gratuitous; it is, as Hegel would say, a free choice that Spirit has made in seeking its self⁄realization.

It would of course be absurd to say that the lives we actually live are controlled by the present⁄day repudiation of the old visionary norm. As householders, housekeepers, and parents we maintain allegiance to it in practice, possibly even in diffident principle. But as *readers*, as participants in the conscious, formulating part of our life in society, we incline to the antagonistic position. When, for example, a gifted novelist, Saul Bellow, tries through his Moses Herzog to question the prevailing negation of the old vision and to assert the value of the achieved and successful life, we respond with discomfort and embarrassment. And the more, no doubt, because we discern some discomfort and embarrassment on the part of Mr. Bellow himself, aris⁄ing from his sufficiently accurate apprehension that in controverting the accepted attitude he lays himself open to

the terrible charge of philistinism, of being a defector from
the ranks of the children of light, a traitor to Spirit. We take
it as an affront to our sense of reality that a contemporary
should employ that mode of judging the spiritual life which
we are willing to accept and even find entrancing when we
encounter it in Shakespeare's romances. Shakespeare un-
abashedly uses material and social establishment and what
it is presumed to assure in the way of order, peace, honour,
and beauty as emblems of the spiritual life, as criteria by
which the sufficiency of the inner condition may be
assessed. He conceives the self in terms of states and activities
which imply achievement and reward, such states as innocence, such activities as repentance and atonement, such
achievement and reward as redemption, 'a clear life ensuing', and even—how astonishing it is!—happiness.[1]

It is this vision of life that Hegel means to discredit when
he speaks with condescension and even contempt of
Diderot-*Moi*. The 'honest soul' is rejected by Hegel because
it is defined and limited by its 'noble' relation to the external
power of society, to the ethos which that power implies.
Nobility has been bourgeoisified in Diderot-*Moi* but not
essentially transmuted. And we of our time, at least as readers,
are, as I say, in essential accord with Hegel's judgement.
We reject the archaic noble vision of life because we desire
to escape the limiting conditions which it imposes. Our
commitment is to such freedom as is to be found in the
exigent spiritual enterprise which, in the English translation
of the *Phenomenology*, goes under the name of 'culture'.

'Culture' is the word chosen to render Hegel's '*Bildung*'.

[1] If we speak of *The Tempest* in the context of a discussion of the *Phenomenology*, we can scarcely fail to remark other elements of the play which bear
in a striking way upon Hegel's formulations—the 'baseness' of Caliban which
commands the sympathy of the modern audience not merely for its pathos
but for what is implied of its 'nobility' by its resistance to servitude, and the
achieved aspiration of Ariel to be Spirit fully realized in autonomy.

In 1910, when J. B. Baillie's version first appeared, the meaning of 'culture' that had been instituted by Matthew Arnold was still in strong force and Baillie felt free to rely on it. He was the more justified in doing so because Arnold clearly had *Bildung* in mind in one of its common meanings when he framed his conception of culture as the development of the self to perfection through its active experience of 'the best that is thought and said in the world'. This sense of the word can now seem only old-fashioned and pious, but this is actually in its favour, for it was exactly Hegel's intention to take his readers aback by making a sanctified word stand for acts of impiety. Culture, as Hegel idiosyncratically defines it, is the characteristic field of experience of the base self; it proposes the activity by which the disintegrated, alienated, and distraught consciousness expresses its negative relation with the external power of society and thereby becomes 'Spirit truly objective', that is, self-determining. The existence of the base self in culture is described as consisting 'in universal talk and in depreciatory judgement which rends and tears everything'. By this activity—base enough in all conscience—whatever is intended 'to signify something real' is broken up, disintegrated. The depreciatory judgement, the malice of universal talk, is said by Hegel to be 'that which in this real world is alone truly of importance'.

This breaking up of everything real, although of definitive importance in the career of Spirit, is anything but a happy activity. The experience of the self in culture is fraught with pain; it entails 'renunciation and sacrifice'. Baillie emphasizes this aspect of culture by a liberty he takes in translating the title of the section of the *Phenomenology* we are considering—for Hegel's '*Der sich entfremdete Geist; die Bildung*', he gives 'Spirit in Self-Estrangement—The Discipline of Culture'. Culture as Hegel conceives it is exactly a discipline in the sense of that word which means inflicted pain. It is by undergoing the pain of culture that the base self is shaped towards nobility, is indeed, Hegel says, already noble.

But of its baseness there is no doubt. The truth of the self, at a certain stage of its historical development, consists in its being *not* true to itself, in there being no self to be true to: the truth for self, for Spirit, consists precisely in deceit and shamelessness. 'The content uttered by Spirit and uttered about itself', Hegel says, 'is . . . the inversion and perversion of all conceptions and realities, a universal deception of itself and others. . . . The shamelessness manifested in stating this deceit is just on that account the greatest truth.' It is therefore not Diderot-*Moi*, not the *philosophe* with his archaic love of simple truth and morality, with his clearly defined self and his commitment to sincerity, who, for Hegel, commands esteem. Rather, it is Rameau, the buffoon, the flattering parasite, the compulsive mimic, without a self to be true to: it is he who represents Spirit moving to its next stage of development.

The high point of Hegel's admiration for Rameau and of his scorn for Diderot is reached in response to the great climax of the dialogue, Rameau's astonishing operatic performance, his momentous abandonment of individuated selfhood to become all the voices of human existence, of all existence. 'He jumbled together thirty different airs, French, Italian, comic, tragic—in every style. Now in a baritone voice he sank to the pit; then straining in falsetto he tore to shreds the upper notes of some air, imitating the while the stance, walk and gestures of the several characters; being in succession furious, mollified, lordly, sneering. First a damsel weeps and he reproduces her kittenish ways; next he is a priest, a king, a tyrant. . . . Now he is a slave, he obeys, calms down, is heartbroken, complains, laughs. . . . With swollen cheeks and sombre throaty sound, he would give us the horns and bassoons. For the oboes he assumed a shrill yet nasal voice, then speeded up the emission of sound to an incredible degree for the strings. . . . He whistled piccolos and warbled traverse flutes, singing, shouting, waving about like a madman, being in himself dancer and ballerina, singer and prima donna, all of them together and the whole orchestra, the whole theatre; then redividing himself into twenty separate roles, running, stopping, glowing at the eyes like one possessed, frothing at the mouth. . . . He was a woman in a spasm of grief, a wretched man sunk in despair, a temple being erected, birds growing silent at sunset, waters murmuring through cool and solitary places or else cascading from a mountaintop, a storm, a hurricane, the anguish of those about to die, mingled with the whistling of the wind and the noise of thunder. He was night and its gloom, shade and silence—for silence itself is depictable in sound. He had completely lost his senses.'

Upon this ultimate impersonation Diderot*Moi* had passed a divided judgement. 'Did I admire? Yes, I did admire. Was I moved to pity? I was moved. But a streak of derision was interwoven with these feelings and denatured them.' And that the rational man can find in the astonishing performance 'a perversion of sentiment with as much shamefulness in it as absolute frankness, candour, and truth', that he should undertake to discriminate the admirable from the contemptible, the noble from the base, is, in Hegel's view, the decisive indication of the undeveloped condition of this 'simple, placid consciousness'.[1]

[1] The passage which Hegel quotes (pp. 544–5) to convey Diderot*Moi*'s judgement of the performance is actually a conflation of two opinions expressed in the dialogue, only one of which (the first I have quoted) refers to the great operaimpersonation; the other refers to an earlier example of Rameau's mimicry, in which Rameau represents himself as a pimp seducing a bourgeois girl on behalf of a wealthy patron.

It should perhaps be remarked that Hegel permits him-self considerable licence in his reading of the dialogue. He praises Rameau's performance because, through its abdica-tion of integral selfhood, it advances Spirit to a 'higher level of conscious life'. 'To be conscious of its own dis-traught and torn existence', he says, 'and to express itself accordingly—this is to pour scornful laughter on existence, on the confusion pervading the whole and on itself as well.' This does not accurately describe the Nephew's perform-ance, which is not scornful but, rather, charged with admiration and love of the human and natural phenomena it represents. Contrary to Hegel's view, there is really not much malice in Rameau; he is by no means identical with Dostoevsky's Underground Man. His performance is an unabashed defence of exactly what the Underground Man disdains, or affects to disdain, the True, the Good, and the Beautiful. For Rameau these make up the Trinity he wor-ships and in whose invincibility he has perfect faith—never, he says, will it be overcome by the forces of darkness. Hegel attributes to him 'the madness of the musician', but Rameau is as much a critical intelligence as Diderot, and when he has finished his intoxicated demonstration of the power of the new art, he conscientiously turns his mind back to the old musical canon to salvage those elements of it which are worthy of continued admiration. As an exemplar of culture he is really rather moderate in his 'rending' and 'tearing' and he shows less 'confusion' than Hegel imputes to him. But such liberties as Hegel takes with Diderot's text are to be noted merely by the way. The dialogue needs no protection from them and may even be thought to welcome them.

This early in our investigation of sincerity we encounter, then, a mind of great authority which proposes to us the dismaying thought that sincerity is undeserving of our respect. I have remarked the obvious connection between sincerity and the intensified sense of personal identity that developed along with the growth of the idea of society. Sincerity was taken to be an element of personal autonomy; as such, it was felt to be what we might call a progressive virtue. But considered in the light of Hegel's historical anthropology, it must be regarded in the opposite way, as regressive and retrospective, looking back to the selfhood of a past time, standing between the self and the disintegra-tion which is essential if it is to develop its true, its entire, freedom.

iii

The dialectical turns and returns of Hegel's *Phenomeno-logy* make esoteric doctrine indeed. Yet in itself the con-ception of the disintegrated, alienated, and distraught consciousness was anything but unfamiliar to the con-temporary audience. It had been the subject of one of the most widely read books of the preceding generation, Goethe's novel *The Sorrows of Young Werther*, which had been published in 1774, at the end of the putative span of years in which *Rameau's Nephew* was written.

I do not know the present status of this remarkable book and whether young readers have to approach it, as they did in my youth, through the ridicule that had been directed to it in Victorian England. George Henry Lewes spoke of the novel's reputation for absurdity among the English— my own first knowledge of the book came to me as a boy from Thackeray's comic verses about Charlotte going on with her cutting bread-and-butter after Werther had blown 'his silly brains out' and was 'borne before her on a shutter'. The reception of the book had been phenomenal

in its enthusiasm—all Europe adored it, and its vogue in
England was for a time scarcely less fervent than on the
Continent. But the Victorians discovered that they had
work to do and the great thing about Werther was that he
did not, which was presumably the case with the young
Germans who were said to have emulated his suicide. The
enlightened English view of the novel in the nineteenth
century was that the emotions it set forth may have been
appropriate to their time but, being childish things, were
to be put away now that maturity had come. So Carlyle
said, and he spoke with the authority of having told, in
Sartor Resartus, the history of his own experience of disintegration, which, unlike Werther's, had been resisted and
overcome. Werther's anguish was real and justified,
Carlyle said, but 'other years and higher culture' had
brought its remedy.

We will be less ready than the Victorians to conclude
that the day of Goethe's youthful novel is over. The greater
historical distance brings the book nearer to us than it was
to them, for it allows us to take in a less literal way than
they did the excesses of sentiment which they found exas-
perating. Beneath all that is adventitious in it, *The Sorrows
of Young Werther* is as hard and enduring as *Rameau's
Nephew* and no less significant in the history of sincerity.

The story falls into two parts. The first is an account of
the hero's effort to ward off the encroachments of disintegration, to remain an honest soul; the second tells of his
free choice of disintegration. Werther, a young and gifted
member of the upper bourgeoisie, hopes to quiet a troubled
state of feeling by living for a time in a pleasant rural
district into which he has come to conclude a matter of
family business. In his early letters to his confidant, Wil-
helm, he gives no reason for his distress of mind, what at
one point he calls his 'seething blood'. And it is quite at

odds with the figure he makes in the world—he conducts himself with the sweetness and decorum of a young prince in a Shakespeare romance, and despite his bourgeois origin he has what Frank Kermode, writing about *The Tempest*, calls the 'magic of nobility', meaning that personal beauty which the romances assign to children of royal stock as the index of their innate virtue: in one of his early letters Werther says, 'I don't know what attraction I must have for people; so many of them like me and attach themselves to me.' And Charlotte, the 'Lotte' with whom he falls in love at their first meeting, has the same magic. In her case, however, personal charm is bound up with doing, with the practical affairs of domesticity. Her mother having recently died, Lotte has charge of her father's house and the rearing of her many brothers and sisters; she fulfils her household duties with the grace that informs her dancing and singing. The lines that are perhaps the loveliest in Shakespeare, Florizel's hymn to Perdita's doing, suggest the charm that Werther finds in Lotte.

> What you do
> Still betters what is done. When you speak, sweet,
> I'd have you do it ever. When you sing,
> I'd have you buy and sell so, so give alms,
> Pray so, and for the ordering your affairs,
> To sing them too. When you do dance, I wish you
> A wave o' th' sea, that you might ever do
> Nothing but that, move still, still so,
> And own no other function. Each your doing,
> So singular in each particular,
> Crowns what you are doing in the present deed
> That all your acts are queens.

It is, as it were, no accident that Lotte's celebrated cutting of bread-and-butter for her little brood takes place just

before she leaves for a dance. The life over which she pre-
sides is as simple and sincere as bread-and-butter and it
seems exactly suited to the needs of Werther's troubled
mind. As, indeed, everything in the district is for a time.
Werther finds a garden to sit in and is charmed by its
simplicity and sincerity—it was laid out 'not by a systematic
gardener but by a feeling heart'. Nature around him is un-
spoiled, mountainous, forested. He reads Homer and is
enchanted by actual scenes of patriarchal life. There are
many children, the very avatars of sincerity; he loves them,
they love him. A young farm labourer adores the widow
who employs him and is happy to think that his feelings
are reciprocated. Lotte tends the sick and elderly; life has
its sadness but grace can comfort it. As Werther says, certain pleasures are still granted to mankind. In his willed
commitment to the condition of the 'honest soul', he makes
what he calls a heartfelt speech against ill humour, which
he says is a disease, a sluggishness of spirit that must be
cured by the activity of work.

Yet his own passions, Werther says, verge upon insanity,
and he means thus to praise them. The archaic world, the
idyllic world of simplicity and sincerity, of life justified, is
after all not for him. His adoration of Lotte cannot express
itself in action: marriage is an estate appropriate to the good,
dull civil servant, Albert, to whom Lotte is betrothed, the
honest consciousness *in excelsis*; for Werther, who is Spirit
seeking its freedom, it is an impossibility.

In the second half of the story, the very nature of the
world changes, as if at the behest of Werther's alienation.
Now the world is no longer of a kind that accommodates
and invites the placid consciousness, the honest soul. All
that was once touched with the archaic nobility now dis-
integrates into baseness. Werther himself loses his 'magic
of nobility', the base world resists his charm—although as

the secretary of a diplomatic legation he associates with his social superiors, the members of an actual if tatty nobility, on one occasion, in absence of mind (so he says), he stays on in the room in which the aristocrats are gathering for their weekly assembly and is snubbed and humiliated by them. This incident is the beginning although not the cause of his despair. Now everything in the external world confirms by its pain and confusion his internal condition. He learns of the death of an infant with whom he had affectionately played. The child's virtuous parents fall into destitution. The amorous farm labourer is thwarted in his love affair and murders his mistress. The glorious nut trees of the parsonage are cut down by the new pastor's bitter-minded wife. 'I am not,' Werther says, 'I am not ever to come to myself.' He has that day encountered a madman in the fields who speaks of a time when he had been happy; the lunatic's mother explains that this was the time when he had been madder still, confined to the madhouse: '*die Zeit, da er von sich war*', the time when he was separated from himself. It is no longer Homer who is Werther's favourite reading but Ossian, the compulsive telling over of defeat, darkness, despair, the eradication of clear outline and all degree, the world torn and scattered.

Only in part does Werther believe that all this observed pain and confusion of existence is accountable for his mounting distraction. It is not through his perception but through his will that the beautiful world of the first half of the novel has yielded place to this world of suffering and nullity. The world as now given is the world as chosen, and the angels might cry to Werther as later they were to cry to Faust: 'Oh, oh! You have destroyed the beautiful world.' The world of order and harmony, of salubrious activity, is the 'noble' world of Diderot-*Moi*, the simple soul, the honest consciousness, the integrated self: only such a self can envision such a world, only such a self can de-light in it. And only such a self can submit to it; Werther cannot, for it is the world of recognized necessity, where, as Hegel put it, Spirit does not exist 'on its own account'.

Werther, of course, does not find freedom through dis-integration; his suicide is not a victory of Spirit but a defeat. If we try to explain his failure in the terms of Hegel's celebration of Rameau, we can say that his alienation did not proceed far enough: he was not able to achieve that detachment from himself which for Hegel constitutes Rameau's triumph and significance. The Nephew de-serves admiration, Hegel says, because through him Spirit is able to pour 'scornful laughter on existence, on the con-fusion pervading the whole and on itself as well'. Spirit is expressed as *esprit*, *Geist* becomes *geistreich*. Werther is in-capable of embodying this desperate cosmic wit; irony is beyond his comprehension. He is in all things the sincere man; even in his disintegration he struggles to be true to the self he must still believe is his own. It is much to the point, especially in the light of Rameau's wild impersona-tions and role-playings, that Werther expresses his sincerity by a singular and apparently unchanging mode of dress—everyone in Europe knew, and many imitated, Werther's costume of dark blue coat, yellow waistcoat, and boots, and Goethe is at pains to mention that it was in this costume that Werther died. To the end and even in his defeat he held fast to the image of a one true self. This tenacity was what had destroyed him. A disintegrated consciousness, he had persisted in clinging to the simplicity of the honest soul.

III · THE SENTIMENT OF BEING
AND THE SENTIMENTS OF ART

i

THE ACCOUNT GIVEN BY HEGEL IN THE *Phenomenology* of the two historic modes of the self, the 'honest soul' and the 'disintegrated consciousness', though it bears upon our contemporary cultural situation with an appositeness which must be immediately and forcibly apparent, has had virtually no currency among students of modern culture who write in English. This curious state of intellectual affairs is probably to be explained by merely adventitious circumstances—by the proverbial difficulty of the *Phenomenology* as a whole and by the compromised repute of its author in British and American academic circles—rather than by any settled disposition to resist the substance of what Hegel says. Actually, indeed, the disposition would seem to be quite the opposite, if we may judge by the peculiar regard in which, over the last fifty years or so, Nietzsche's *Birth of Tragedy* has come to be held and the ready response given to its exposition of the Apollonian and Dionysian principles. These, to be sure, are not historic modes of the self, but, rather, eternal modes of art and existence. Yet they are obviously cognate with the 'honest soul' and the 'disintegrated consciousness' and the welcome which they have been given suggests that Hegel's concepts might well be found equally cogent. The Apollonian principle is that of positive ends in view, of manifest reason and order. It is associated with light, vision, and the plastic arts. The Dionysian principle is its negation. It seeks to destroy limits and distinctions. It is indifferent to pleasure and pain, its good is ecstasy and the extinction of the individuated self. Its characteristic art is music, or at least such music as overbears and dissolves the sense of self.

When we attempt to trace the history of the self, we of course know that we are dealing with shadows in a dark land. Our predications must be diffident, our conclusions can be only speculative. And yet we cannot withhold all confidence from the impression that in our time the conflict between the 'honest soul' and the 'disintegrated consciousness' has moved towards overtness, that the dialectic between the Apollonian and the Dionysian principles has altered its ancient terms. Our proper scepticism cannot wholly discount the evidence that the conception of the self has been undergoing a drastic revision, of which a notable element is the lessening of the value formerly assigned to its individuation. There are, for example, few contemporary readers of *The Birth of Tragedy* who really hold with Nietzsche's doctrine that tragedy is the outcome of a true dialectic between Apollo and Dionysus—Dionysus is commonly taken to be the protagonist of the great essay, the essential genius of tragedy, while Apollo figures as a rather tiresome ancillary character whose job it is to busy himself with the mere practical details of form. Nietzsche explicitly cautions us against taking this biased view, yet he himself is in part responsible for it: his own excitement over the discovery of the Dionysian principle is infectious.

Any discerning account of the artistic enterprise of recent decades is bound to bring us word of some defeat suffered by the 'honest soul'. A book by Wylie Sypher gives a pretty full report in its very title, *Loss of Self in Modern*

Literature and Art. Professor Sypher tells us that the ideal which goes under the name of humanism is perhaps in some degree still viable, but only if we do not involve it with the kind of selfhood which he calls 'romantic individuality', for, he says, 'The image of the self held in past eras has been effaced from the universe. . . .'

The news of the effacement of this old image is lent confirmation by what we hear of the deserved fate of psychology. We are instructed by certain novelists and critics that psychology has no validity, or none for literature, and that the introduction of psychology into the novel can only be— perhaps has always been—a corruption of the genre's purity. This puzzles us, at least if we are of a certain age. The image of the self we were brought up to hold would seem to imply, even to depend on, there being such a thing as psychology. We know we have psyches because they make trouble for us—our most constant and reliable awareness of selfhood derives from the experience of that trouble. Having been led to believe that the novel characteristically deals with people who have selves substantially like our own, we can only wonder what a literary theorist such as Alain Robbe-Grillet means when he says that if the novel is to survive, it must renounce its old commitment to psychology. And yet only a little effort of honesty is needed for us to recognize how bored we are by detailed exposition of the psychological processes when we meet it in contemporary fiction. We are wearied by it, perhaps not instantly and consciously, but eventually and essentially. While we were reading, say, Philip Roth's *Portnoy's Complaint*, we were no doubt engaged by it, but were we not finally indifferent to all that to-do on the analyst's couch about the emotional consequences of having a mother, of being Jewish, of belonging to this or that inferior class, about what is or is not normal healthy sexuality and what fosters or prevents it? Whatever considerations of this kind may still mean to us within the four walls of our private lives, as the material of art they seem no longer to make their old claim upon the imagination.

And even in our private lives the importance of these and related concerns would appear to be not what it once was. Anna Freud, in the course of a lecture delivered on the 112th anniversary of her father's birth, remarked on the extent to which the young are now alienated from psycho-analysis. Miss Freud did no more than summarily note the cultural fact; she made no attempt to explain it. But surely a partial explanation is not hard to come by. When Freud's thought was first presented to a scandalized world, the recognition of unconditioned instinctual impulse which lies at its core was erroneously taken to mean that Freud wished to establish the dominion of impulse, with all that this implies of the negation of the socialized self. But then of course it came to be understood that the bias of psycho-analysis, so far from being Dionysian, is wholly in the ser-vice of the Apollonian principle, seeking to strengthen the 'honest soul' in the selfhood which is characterized by purposiveness and a clear-eyed recognition of limits. The adverse judgement increasingly passed upon psycho-analysis, and not by the young alone, not only expresses an antagonism to its normative assumptions and to the social conformity which is believed to inhere in its doc-trine, but is also an affirmation of the unconditioned nature of the self, of its claim to an autonomy so complete that all systematic predications about it are either offensively reduc-tive, or gratuitously prescriptive, or irrelevant.

The evidence is indeed abundant that Hegel was right when he envisaged the developing hegemony of the 'dis-integrated consciousness' and consigned the 'honest soul' to the contempt of history. And his prescience will appear the more remarkable when we reflect on how long a cast his prophecy made from the manifest state of spiritual affairs in the age in which he wrote. The social and political world of that age was shaped by and for the 'honest soul'. It is of course true that the 'disintegrated consciousness' lurked subversively about the fortresses of the 'honest soul', and upon its brilliant, desperate assaults the historian of literature and culture habitually focuses his attention. But it was the 'honest soul' that had built the fortresses and then busied itself to make them impregnable. 'Close thy Byron; open thy Goethe'—in that celebrated injunction of Car⁄lyle's we find the manifest ruling intention of the age. Carlyle meant the Byron of the early *Childe Harold* and of *Manfred*; he did not mean the Goethe of *The Sorrows of Young Werther* except as Goethe himself understood that work to be the record of a pathology from which he had had to recover before, as Carlyle put it, 'he could become a man'. Carlyle was invoking a morally affirmative Goethe for whom 'striving' was a guarantee of salvation and re⁄nunciation the law of life. This was the working Goethe, the culture⁄hero with positive practical ends in view. Matthew Arnold had no great regard for Carlyle's way of looking at things, but the two men were at one in their admiration of Goethe. They conceived his greatness to lie in his resemblance to the very universe itself, which was, they were confident, an 'honest soul' of a universe, having its own positive ends in view and characterized by the sincerity of strenuous effort.

Professor Henri Peyre, in his compendious *Literature and Sincerity*, says in effect that sincerity is to be thought of as pre⁄eminently a French concept because of the long intense preoccupation with it that the French have shown. It is an extravagant idea, yet it serves to suggest that there are national differences in sincerity and that a distinction is to be made between the French and the English mode. In French literature sincerity consists in telling the truth about oneself to oneself and to others; by truth is meant a recognition of such of one's own traits or actions as are morally or socially discreditable and, in conventional course, concealed. English sincerity does not demand this confrontation of what is base or shameful in oneself. The English ask of the sincere man that he communicate without deceiving or misleading. Beyond this what is required is only a single-minded commitment to whatever dutiful enterprise he may have in hand. Not to know oneself in the French fashion and make public what one knows, but to be oneself, in action, in deeds, what Matthew Arnold called 'tasks'—this is what the English sincerity consists in.

One of the decisive cultural events of the modern epoch was the conflation of these two national sincerities, the French and the English, in the temperament of a Swiss. Rousseau begins his *Confessions* with the brag that his French sincerity is unique in its perfection. 'I have resolved on an enterprise which has no precedent and which, once complete, will have no imitator. My purpose is to display to my kind a portrait in every way true to nature, and the man I portray will be myself.' At the last trumpet, he says, he will be able to present himself before his Sovereign Judge holding that book in which he has displayed himself as good, generous, and noble, but also as vile and despicable. 'So let the numberless legion of my fellow men gather round me and hear my confessions. Let them groan at my depravities and blush for my misdeeds. But let each one of them reveal his heart at the foot of thy throne with equal sincerity, and may any man who dares say, "I was a better man than he." '

On his pre-eminence in sincerity Rousseau is uncompromising. The claims of his likeliest rival are dismissed out of hand—his expressions of scorn for the show of sincerity made by Montaigne are recurrent and unqualified. 'I have always been amused', he says grandly, 'at Montaigne's false ingenuousness and at his pretence of confessing his faults while taking good care to admit only likeable ones; whereas I, who believe, and always have believed, that I am on the whole the best of men, felt that there is no human breast, however pure, that does not conceal some odious vice.'[1] About his own truth-telling he says no more than the truth. He does not shrink from injuring himself in the world's eyes. We do not easily come to terms with the sloven self-regard of Rousseau's youth; his sexual perversities are not appealing; some of the things which he confesses to having done on impulse—deserting the travelling companion who suffered an epileptic fit in the street of a strange town at night, accusing the good chambermaid of possessing the ribbon that he himself had stolen—are repellent in their baseness.

He speaks of himself as *une âme déchirée*. The phrase is a pretty literal equivalent of 'disintegrated consciousness' and he did indeed display the traits which Hegel attributes to that consciousness, including the simultaneous courting and transcendence of shame. That he set store by the disintegration we cannot doubt: he believed that it, and not wholeness of spirit, offered the path to knowledge. But at the same time he aspired to the 'honest soul' in its wholeness; it was in the single-minded performance of appointed 'tasks' that he discovered the principle of man's earthly

[1] In her 'Rousseau and Montaigne' (Columbia University dissertation, 1968, pp. 127–8), Ellen S. Silber says, 'In the introduction to the 1764 manuscript of *Les Confessions*, Rousseau's remarks about Montaigne's lack of sincerity constitute a full-fledged attack on the essayist's good faith.' The tenor of these remarks is suggested by the first sentence of the passage that Dr. Silber quotes: '*Je mets Montaigne à la tête de ces faux sincères qui veulent tromper en disant vrai.*'

salvation. What I have called English sincerity was at the heart of Rousseau's political thought.

The work which won for Rousseau his initial fame was the so-called *First Discourse*, to which the concept of sincerity is central. The essay responds to the question proposed by the Academy of Dijon—'Has the restoration of the sciences and the arts tended to purify morals?' We know, of course, that it answers in the negative, but when we undertake to paraphrase Rousseau's argument without having the text before us, we find it hard to do so with accuracy—the chances are that we will assign to the phrase 'the sciences and the arts' a unitary and general meaning and make it stand for civilization as a whole, and understand Rousseau to be saying that civilization, so far from purifying morals, has corrupted the elemental, essential nature of man. This formulation is not alien to Rousseau's intention, but it is not what he says in the *First Discourse*. What he does say goes so much against our settled views that we cannot readily accept that he really does say it. The proposition he advances is that the practice of the sciences and the arts is a peculiarly corrupting aspect of civilization. His emphasis is upon the arts, by which he chiefly means literature. It is literature that is the pre-eminent agent of man's corruption, the essence or paradigm of the inherent falsehood of civilized society. Literature embodies the very principle of society, which is the individual's abnegation of personal autonomy in order to win the forbearance and esteem of others—early in the *First Discourse* Rousseau says that the chief usefulness literary occupations may be thought to have is that 'they make men more sociable [read: more conformable] by inspiring in them the desire to please one another with works worthy of their mutual approval'.

We are habituated to the idea that society, though necessary for survival, corrupts the life it fosters, and most of us give this idea some degree of assent. But we receive with no such tolerance the idea that literature is an accomplice in the social betrayal. This offends our deepest pieties. And in defence of the art we love and trust we seize eagerly upon Rousseau's statement that literature is motivated by the desire to 'please', that it is characterized by a 'uniform and false veil of politeness' and by 'that much vaunted urbanity which we owe to the enlightenment of our century'—it is plain, we say, that Rousseau takes an all too local and temporal view of literature; the intention of the great works of the past, let alone of the age to come, is surely not comprised by the simple and servile purpose of 'pleasing'. The literature to which we give our admiration and gratitude fulfils its function exactly by rending the false veil of politeness, by refusing the compromises of urbanity.

This objection serves our piety but it does not really confront what Rousseau is saying about literature. It is true that he frames his indictment in terms of a particular aesthetic doctrine instituted in the Renaissance, still ascendant in his own day, and now wholly without credit. But his concern is far from being anachronistic: its real object is the developing status of literature in the modern world, its relation to that new social circumstance of which I have spoken, the ever more powerful existence of the *public*, that human entity which is defined by its urban habitat, its multitudinousness, and its ready accessibility to opinion. The individual who lives in this new circumstance is subject to the constant influence, the literal *in-flowing*, of the mental processes of others, which, in the degree that they stimulate or enlarge his consciousness, make it less his own. He finds it ever more difficult to know what his own self is and what being true to it consists in. It is with the psychological and moral consequences of the modern public dispensation in mind that Rousseau invents his famous savage, one of whose defining traits is the perfect autonomy of his consciousness. 'The savage lives within himself,' Rousseau says in the *Second Discourse*; 'the sociable man knows how to live only in the opinion of others, and it is, so to speak, from their judgement alone that he draws the sentiment of his own being.' In Rousseau's view, literature stands pre-eminent among the agencies of modern society which convey opinion and make it forcible and thus control and qualify the individual's sentiment of his own being.

As the case against literature is argued in the *First Discourse*, the generality and abstractness of its terms might make it seem merely captious. But eight years later, in 1758, Rousseau returned to the charge in a work which is specific and concrete almost to the point of compulsiveness. In the *Letter to M. d'Alembert on the Theatre* Rousseau considers the particular evils which would follow from the introduction of a literary genre, the drama, into a given society, one which he judges to be as satisfactory as a modern society can be, that of his native Geneva. It is a bourgeois society of considerable prosperity; the form of its political organization is republican. For Rousseau the admirable aspect of Geneva lies in the contrast between its morals and manners and those of Paris. Despite the prosperity it has achieved, its mode of life has certain qualities that are commonly found and admired in far simpler communities —for example, there prevails among its citizens a high degree of the fraternal feeling that Lévi-Strauss observes and celebrates in some of the tribes of *Tristes Tropiques*. Rousseau sets especial store by the effect on the city's social and moral tone of the so-called 'circles', small clubs of men organized for conviviality and sport.[1] D'Alembert had expressed the

---

[1] The anti-Parisian and anti-modern tendency of the *Letter to M. d'Alembert* shows itself in nothing so much as in its resistance to the influence of women. It cannot be called anti-feminine, but its conception of the sexes and of the right relation between them harks back, as does much else in the work, to Sparta.

view in his *Encyclopédie* article on Geneva that the general amenity of the city required for its completeness the establishment of a theatre. This suggestion Rousseau repels with rational indignation. The objection he offers to the dramatic art is essentially the one he had advanced in the *First Discourse* against literature in general, that it reduces the actuality and autonomy of the self.

The claim made for the theatre that it advances moral enlightenment is met by Rousseau with impatient incredulity. The purpose of the theatre is to please, and such moral judgement as it makes is accepted to the extent that it is pleasurable, which is to say, so far as it confirms and flatters the settled views of the audience. The general effect of the theatre is not to correct but 'to augment the natural inclinations, and to give new energy to all the passions'. With the theory of tragic catharsis, which was coming to hold a sanctified place in aesthetic–moral thought, Rousseau will have no truck; the idea that the theatre purges the passions by exciting them is, he says, beyond his comprehension and can scarcely have been put forward in good faith—'Is it possible that in order to be temperate and prudent, we must begin by being intemperate and mad?'

'I suspect', he says at one point, 'that any man to whom the crimes of Phaedra or Medea were told beforehand would hate them more at the beginning of the play than at the end.' Rousseau's scepticism about the direct moral effect of tragedy prepares the way for Nietzsche's statement that tragedy proposes man's metaphysical destiny of transcending morality. This, of course, is an idea which Rousseau himself could not possibly have entertained—despite all that he says about the corruption that society works upon man, his whole sense of man's destiny is bounded by the social life, which, as he conceives it, depends for its right existence upon the urgent moral rectitude of the simple

soul. The theatre sophisticates simplicity and for moral
rectitude it substitutes a self-deceiving moral sensibility.
'When a man has gone to admire fine actions in stories and
to cry for imaginary miseries, what more can be asked of
him? Is he not satisfied with himself? Does he not applaud
his fine soul? Has he not acquitted himself of all that he
owes to virtue by the homage which he has just rendered
it?'

The spectator, we might put it, contracts by infection
the characteristic disease of the actor, the attenuation of
selfhood that results from impersonation. Rousseau's
condemnation of the actor's trade is similar to Plato's but
not exactly the same. Plato said that the soul of the actor
is deteriorated by identification with such morally inferior
characters as he impersonates: the role of a slave induces
servility, that of a woman effeminacy, that of a villain
wickedness. The professional deformation that Rousseau
deplores is that by engaging in impersonation at all the
actor diminishes his own existence as a person: his is the
art of 'counterfeiting himself, of putting on another character than his own'.[1] And what the actor suffers in an

[1] The classic argument against the view that the actor is personally affected,
let alone deteriorated, by his assumption of roles is made by Diderot in *Paradoxe
sur le comédien*, written between 1775 and 1778 but not published until 1830.
I am grateful to Theodore Ziolkowski for suggesting to me that Rousseau's
strictures on the acting profession ought to be considered with reference to the
revolt against the established rhetorical style of acting, with its six conventional
gestures, which took place in France and Germany around 1750. In his
paper 'Language and Mimetic Action in Lessing's *Miss Sara Sampson*' (*The
Germanic Review*, Nov. 1965, 262-76), Professor Ziolkowski says that among
the innovators it was a matter for debate whether the naturalness they desired
was best achieved by the actor producing 'within himself the emotion that he
is supposed to represent on the stage', expecting the appropriate gestures and
facial expressions to follow, or, on the contrary, by the actor remaining 'cool
and objective' and mastering 'a variety of physical techniques in the hope of
dissembling emotion he does not feel'. The debate, of course, continues into
our day.

extreme degree, is in some measure suffered by the spectator, as, to use a modern word, he empathizes with the
character on the stage.

Rousseau is at pains to make it clear that his opposition
to the theatre is based on no puritanical dislike of pleasure,
only on his perception of the extent to which the theatrical
art falsifies the self and thus contributes to the weakening
of society. 'What!', he asks, 'are there to be no entertainments in a republic?', and at once makes answer, 'On the
contrary, there ought to be many. . . .' The entertainments
appropriate to a republic are those in which the citizen,
participating in his own person, is reinforced in the sentiment of his own being and in his relation to his fellow
beings. 'People think that they come together in the theatre
and it is there that they are isolated. It is there that they go
to forget their friends, neighbours, and relations in order to
concern themselves with fables, in order to cry for the mis-
fortunes of the dead or to laugh at the expense of the living.'
In the place of 'exclusive entertainments which close up a
small number of people in melancholy fashion in a gloomy
cavern, which keeps them fearful and immobile in silence
and inaction', there are to be free and festive gatherings
'in the open air, under the sky' at which nothing will
be *shown*. The incidents of these occasions of happy
communality will be games and athletic contests, regattas,
reviews, and the ceremonies of prize-giving. 'Let the
spectators become an entertainment to themselves; make
them actors themselves; do it so that each one sees and
loves himself in the others.'

Only a few years ago the response to Rousseau's view of
artistic culture would have been more clearly negative than
it is today, when in some quarters it is believed that 'showing' is to be repudiated in favour of participation, exactly
to the end of loving ourselves in others. Still, the pieties

about art to which most of us have been bred will incline
us to agree with Peter Gay when, in his book on the
Enlightenment, he says that this is 'Rousseau at his most
unpleasant'. Which is to say, Rousseau moralistic, utilitarian, indifferent to the 'sensibilities' which art helps us
cultivate. As Professor Gay goes on to remark, even if it
did not put us in mind of the cultural programmes of
totalitarian societies, this aspect of Rousseau's thought is
distasteful. No doubt. But our ready dislike of it must not
lead us to overlook an important part of Rousseau's intention which is not moralistic and utilitarian but in itself
aesthetic, although the beauty to which it refers is not that
of artistic products but of actual persons. Rousseau is concerned to foster a human type whose defining characteristic
is autonomy, the will and strength to make strict choice
among the elements of our enforced life in society. Put it
that he is aesthetically revolted by the trashiness of what,
some twenty years ago, David Riesman called the 'other-
directed' personality, which he saw as becoming ever more
salient in our society. This is the personality whose whole
being is attuned to catch the signals sent out by the consensus of his fellows and by the institutional agencies of
the culture, to the extent that he is scarcely a self at all, but,
rather, a reiterated impersonation. On this score it is surely
possible for us to be in accord with Rousseau. We too have
a predilection for the self-sufficiency and self-definition of
the two other types of personality that Professor Riesman
described, the archaic type he calls 'inner-directed', which
has at least the appearance and ideal of autonomy, and the
hypothetical type which is truly self-directed.

But one of our most esteemed certitudes, firmly established in our advanced educational system, is that personal
autonomy is fostered by art. Rousseau says just the opposite.
Twenty years ago it would have seemed absurd of anyone

to question that cherished belief of ours, and even now it seems vicious to stand it on its head and to say, as Rousseau does, that art is one of the agents of conformity, that it is hostile to the sentiment of one's own existence. Inferior art, commercial-popular art, has always been thought corrupting. But serious art, by which we mean such art as stands, overtly or by implication, in an adversary relation to the dominant culture—surely on this ground or nowhere a man can set up the smithy in which to forge his autonomous selfhood? Yet at the present time certain developments in the ecology of art must make us less confident of this than we once were. The unprecedented proliferation of art, the ease with which formerly esoteric or repellent art-forms are accepted, the fascinating conjunction of popular and commercial art with what used to be called advanced art—these circumstances do not support the old belief that art fosters a personal autonomy. Say, if you like, that art conducts to the individual certain of the more rarefied cultural energies, moves him in certain hitherto untaken directions, offers him such confirmation of the sense of individuality as may be found in social enclaves organized around aesthetic preferences. But this is not autonomy: the rule, the law, derives from others. Rousseau, living in an age when the new opinion-forming power of art could already be discerned, says nothing more, nor less, than this.

ii

In his general condemnation of literature there are two literary genres which Rousseau holds blameless because they do not sophisticate the integrity of the honest soul nor diminish its sincerity. One of these genres is oratory, the other is the novel.

The first exemption is of course not surprising. A republic can scarcely dispense with oratory, and the orator is not—so Rousseau tells us—susceptible to the corrupting influence of impersonation since, unlike the actor, 'he fills only his own role . . . , speaks only in his own name'. But we are bound to be astonished at Rousseau's belief that the novel suits the republican character and that, unlike the drama, it does not threaten the simplicity and integrity of the self. The desolate ghost of poor Emma Bovary rises up to pro-test that the opposite is so, that, even more than the theatre, the novel seduces the self to role-playing, to fantasy and impersonation. To which, for the moment at least, the reply may be that Rousseau's experience was different: his own self in its integrity was formed, he believed, by night-long bouts of novel-reading with his father when he was five or six years old. It was from these, he said, that he dated 'the unbroken sentiment of his being'.

Oratory and the novel: which is to say, Robespierre and Jane Austen.

This, I fancy, is the first time the two personages have ever been brought together in a single sentence, separated from each other by nothing more than the conjunction that links them. They have not been factitiously conjoined: they are consanguineous, each is in lineal descent from Rousseau, cousins-german through their commitment to the 'honest soul' and its appropriate sincerity.

Writers on Robespierre frequently sum up the whole of his intellectual life and much of his temperament by refer-ence to the strength of his devotion to Rousseau, which began in his schooldays. Through all his career, says his English biographer, J. M. Thompson, 'he was as sincere, as solemn, and as self-questioning as his master, the model of Jacobinism, Jean-Jacques Rousseau'. Albert Mathiez speaks of the 'profound sincerity' which 'touched and sub-jugated the Assembly'. The sincerity was not doubted even by his most implacable enemies. The Seagreen Incorrup-tible—so Carlyle delighted to call him in mockery of his conscious rectitude and the dandified colour of his coat—is Molière's Alceste in a third avatar, Rousseau himself, as we saw, having been the second. Yet this most militantly sincere and single-minded of honest souls became in the literal sense of the word a hypocrite, which is to say an actor, the leading player in a comedy of principle, perfidy, and blood. Neither the admiration that Robespierre in some measure deserves, nor the horror he inspires, nor the ghastliness of his end, can dispel the comic aura in which he stands before us, in this respect unique among world-historical figures.

Hannah Arendt, in her book *On Revolution*, gives a subtle and impassioned account of the moral disposition of Robespierre, laying particular emphasis upon the theatrical character which he shared with all the men who, as she puts it, 'enacted the Revolution'. Their rhetoric was con-sciously that of the theatre, to which their metaphors made specific reference. It is of course the tragic or heroic theatre that Dr. Arendt refers to, yet when she says that the men of the Revolution conceived it to be their historic mission 'to tear the mask of hypocrisy off the face of French society', it is a scene from comedy that springs to mind. The revolu-tionary preoccupation with the hypocrisy of the old French society resulted in an obsessive concern with the possible—the all too probable—hypocrisy of the individual, even of one's own self. The Revolution brought to its highest in-tensity the idea of the public, and established, Dr. Arendt suggests, an ultimate antagonism between the unshadowed manifestness of the public life and the troubled ambiguity of the personal life, the darkness of man's unknowable heart. What was private and unknown might be presumed to be subversive of the public good. From this presumption grew the preoccupation with sincerity, with the necessity of expressing and guaranteeing it to the public —sincerity required a rhetoric of avowal, the demonstration of single-minded innocence through attitude and posture, exactly the role-playing in which Rousseau had found the essence of personal, ultimately of social, corruption. 'One cannot', André Gide has said, 'both be sincere and seem so.'

Molière had proposed something close to this. Alceste's proud claim to a perfect sincerity encroaches upon the darkness of the unknowable heart. The absoluteness of his undertaking not to be false to any man leads to the extirpation of most of the self to which he is determined to be true. So too with Robespierre. But History's version of the comedy is more elaborate than Molière's. It is not merely that Robespierre extirpates the dark, ambiguous self but that in its place he establishes a self of his own devising, made up of elements derived from various personages who had figured, to popular acclaim, on the stage of History, Rousseau being one among them. Alceste, unwilling to be implicated in the darkness and ambiguity of society, banished himself from his kind to live in solitude and silence. Robespierre lives and moves and has his devised being in full view of the public to which he directs his unceasing voice. His last great comic moment before his fall was an occasion in which virtually the whole population of Paris participated, some half-million people—society transfigured into the public, its darkness and ambiguity thus overcome, its motives all clear and avowed to itself and to the watching world.

This was the famous Festival of the Supreme Being of 8 June 1793, in which, as ordained by the Convention,

the French nation dedicated itself to the theistic creed of
Rousseau's Savoyard Vicar. Whether by intention or in-
advertence, the day appointed for the festival was Whit-
sunday, which, in the calendar of the displaced Church,
commemorates the descent of the Holy Spirit.[1] The celebration reached its climax on the Champs de Mars, renamed
the Champs de la Réunion, where the people stood massed
before its legislators, who were seated on the artificial
mound that symbolized the 'Mountain' of the Convention;
it was crowned by a Tree of Liberty. Robespierre presided,
holding in his hand a bouquet of flowers and an ear of
wheat. There were many speeches and the vast assemblage
was led first in a hymn to the Being whose existence it
was ratifying and then in patriotic songs. Multitude and
unanimity proved intoxicating; to salvoes of artillery and
with cries of '*Vive la République!*', fervent embraces were
exchanged. The enormous public act of faith had been
inaugurated by Robespierre that morning in the ceremony
in the Tuileries Gardens. Here the representatives of the
people and the national deputies had met, arrayed in their
brilliant new official dress, carrying flowers, wheat, and
fruit. To them Robespierre, as President of the Convention, had delivered an oration in praise of theism, at the
conclusion of which he set fire to an effigy of Atheism,
from whose ashes there emerged, by means of machinery,
the image of Wisdom, unfortunately a little scorched by
the flames. The whole magniloquent occasion had been
designed, directed, and rehearsed by David and was
judged to be his finest achievement in this line of
work.

The ironies of that great day of public self-realization and
self-congratulation are classic in their grandiosity, precision,
and clarity—it could only be banal, not to say cruel, to

[1] The liturgical colour of this feast is red.

explicate the doubt they cast upon Rousseau's confidence that oratory is a literary genre which is immune to the corruption inherent in impersonation.

What, then, of the other licensed genre, the novel? What of the novelist, to whom, together with Robespierre, I have ascribed a lineal descent from Rousseau?

Jane Austen never mentions Rousseau in her letters, and although there is ground for believing that she read *La Nouvelle Héloïse*, it is unlikely that her acquaintance with him went beyond this one work. It is not, however, an influence that I would propose, but, rather, an affinity, a common concern for the defence of the 'honest soul', with its definitive quality of single-mindedness and sincerity.

Two passages from Rousseau will serve to suggest the nature of the affinity. The first occurs in the *Letter to M. d'Alembert*. In the course of explaining the salubrious effects of the novel, Rousseau says that it is the English novel he has in mind, of which some examples are no doubt detestable, but which at its best is sublime, its best being *Clarissa*. The *Letter* was written before Rousseau had become embittered at the English by his disastrous visit among them, and he ascribes to the English aristocracy certain traits which make it admirable by comparison with the French. English ladies, for example, share many of the characteristics of the best of their male compatriots; they have a degree of Spartan simplicity which permits their sentiment of being, their sense of selfhood, to depend on themselves, not on the opinion of others. The solitude of their great parks does not frighten but pleases them. They are, in short, not Parisians; *le tout Paris* does not determine their being. 'From this common taste for solitude arises a taste for contemplative reading and the novels with which England is inundated. Thus both [sexes], withdrawn more and more into themselves, give themselves less to frivolous imitations, get more of a taste for the true pleasures of life, and think less of appearing happy than of being so.'

I shall again avoid the question of whether the genre of the novel does in fact inculcate and sustain the autonomy of the self or whether it perhaps does just the opposite, leading the self into factitiousness. Rousseau's own experience, as we have seen, was that from novel-reading he had derived the sentiment of his being, in which he found nothing less than the meaning of life, the reason for existence: the sentiment of being, he was to say in the *Rêveries*, brought 'a contentment and peace which alone would suffice to make this existence sweet and dear'.

The sentiment of being, it need scarcely be said, is the criterion by which Jane Austen judges the quality of the selves she brings into her purview. Whoever in her novels wins her regard—her compassionate or comic indulgence is another thing—possesses in a high degree the sentiment of being, with all that this implies of self-sufficiency, self-definition, and sincerity. So far as it is indeed a sentiment, her women are likely to possess it in a higher degree than her men, just as in Shakespeare's romances it is the princesses rather than the princes who best embody the quality of life that the plays celebrate. In Jane Austen's novels, as in Shakespeare's late plays, the character of the heroines is shaped by their spirited acquiescence in the societal mode that Hegel called 'noble' and represented as the definitive circumstance of the 'honest soul'. Its visionary norm of life is the order, peace, honour, and beauty which inhere in a happy and (as used to be said) prosperous marriage, in the sufficiency and decorum of fortunate domestic arrangements. Nothing in the novels questions the ideal of the archaic 'noble' life which is appropriate to the great and beautiful houses with the ever-remembered names—Northanger Abbey, Donwell Abbey, Pemberley,

Hartfield, Kellynch Hall, Norland Park, Mansfield Park. In them 'existence is sweet and dear', at least if one is rightly disposed; they hold nothing less than the meaning of life for those who are fitted to seek it and to cherish it when it is found. With what the great houses represent the heroines of the novels are, or become, wholly in accord. Their aspiration reaches no further. Doubtless this was what Emerson had in mind when he expressed his detestation of Jane Austen's novels for their 'sterility' and 'vulgarity'.

It is far from being the judgement that Rousseau would have made. We have seen that, for all the great part he had in bringing the modern world into being, for all that the tendency of his thought is subversive of the old order, he regarded the emerging new world with intense anxiety, and exactly because it was in process of destroying the old 'noble' life. Despite his concern with equality, his ideal of the good life was shaped by his taste for the aristocratic mode; he never repudiated the fantasy of it from which he took courage at a crucial moment of his troubled adolescence.[1] He speaks of this touching dream in the *Confessions*, in the second of the two passages which I said bore upon the affinity between him and Jane Austen. The engraver's apprentice, sixteen years old, has resolved to run away from his master and his native city to seek his fortune in the world and Rousseau recalls with tender irony the terms of happiness which the boy stipulates. 'My expectations', he says, 'were not boundless. One charming circle would be enough; more would be an embarrassment. Modestly I imagined myself one of a narrow but exquisitely chosen clan, over which I felt confident I would rule. A single

[1] For a useful account of Rousseau's personal preferences in class-determined modes of life, see Roger D. Masters, *The Political Philosophy of Rousseau* (Princeton, N.J., 1968), p. 428 n.

castle was the limit of my ambition. To be the favourite of its lord and lady, the lover of their daughter, the friend of their son, and the protector of their neighbours: that would be enough; I required no more.' He wished, in short, to be Fanny Price in Mansfield Park, not, of course, in her creep⁄mouse days, but in her time of flowering, when her full worth is known and her single⁄mindedness and sin⁄ cerity have made her loved by all.[1]

How right, then, that *Mansfield Park* should contain its own 'Letter on the Theatre'. Everyone remembers having been puzzled or exasperated, or both, by the novel's elaborate to⁄do over the amateur theatricals to which the young people devote themselves during the absence of the master of Mansfield Park, Sir Thomas Bertram, and the unequivocal judgement the novel makes that the enterprise is to be deplored. The objection to the histrionic art is exactly Rousseau's: impersonation leads to the negation of self, thence to the weakening of the social fabric.[2] The bluff, unimaginative single⁄mindedness of Sir Thomas is not in every way admirable—it is explicitly blamed for the bad rearing of the two Bertram girls, which has resulted in their ugly personal qualities and empty lives—yet it is the

[1] In associating Rousseau's 'taste for the aristocratic mode' with the life that Jane Austen depicts, I of course don't mean to suggest that the personages of her novels are members of the nobility.

[2] This at the time was scarcely a unique or eccentric view. Although in 1634 the Egerton family thought it quite in order that the young daughter of the house should play the Lady in *Comus*, defending her chastity from the specious persuasions of lust, in the early nineteenth century the serious upper⁄ class view of amateur theatricals was less lenient. Thackeray makes it charac⁄ teristic of Becky Sharp that she figures in them with great success. In Disraeli's *The Young Duke* a fashionable lady of questionable principles mocks the idea that they are in any way objectionable. John Monckton Milnes is warned by his father that taking part in country⁄house 'mimes' tends to lower a man in public respect. In America, in the early years of the twentieth century, the same judgement was in force—the downfall of Lily Bart, the heroine of Edith Wharton's *The House of Mirth*, begins with her success in private theatricals.

principle on which Mansfield Park is founded and by which it endures and holds out its promise of order, peace, honour, and beauty.

Mansfield Park is notoriously an exception among Jane Austen's novels in the sternness, even the harshness, with which it judges the tendencies that threaten the 'noble' mode of life and the 'honest soul'. The once common view was that, although her characters are rooted in social actuality, Jane Austen does not conceive of society as being in any sense problematical, as making issues by reason of the changes it was undergoing in her time. In the present state of opinion about the novelist there is little disposition to accept this. On the contrary, a large part of the interest of her work is now thought to lie exactly in the sensitivity of her response to social change. This she envisages much as Rousseau and Hegel do, not directly and in its gross mani-festations but in terms of the new consciousness with which —whether as cause or as effect—it is associated, a conscious-ness characterized by its departure from singleness and simplicity, by the negation of self through role-playing, by commitment to an artistic culture and what this entails of alienation from the traditional ethos. To none of the traits of the new consciousness does Jane Austen give her approval. But the judgement she passes on them is not merely adverse. Except in one instance, which will be noted, she judges not as Rousseau does, categorically, but as Hegel does, dialectically. She has no doubt that the behaviour of Marianne Dashwood and Emma Wood-house deserves reproof, yet at the same time she salutes it as the effort of Spirit to resist the conditions imposed upon it by the 'noble' ethos, moving, if not through 'baseness', then at least through vanity and imprudence, towards the new 'nobility' of autonomy. Typically in Jane Austen's novels the archaic ethos is in love with the consciousness that seeks to subvert it. There is no more momentous scene in English fiction than that in which Marianne Dashwood's alienated spirit, her hope of making a wild dedication of herself to unpathed waters, undreamed shores, is justified by the sudden sympathy and even admiration which her dutiful sister Elinor gives to the distraught consciousness of Marianne's lover, the faithless and destructive Willoughby. If Mr. Knightley does not set himself at a hopeless distance from us by being exemplary in his station and the discharge of its duties but, on the contrary, engages our liking, it is because we perceive that he cherishes Emma not merely in spite of her subversive self-assertion but because of it. Little Catharine Morland is silly and even vulgar in her prying into the fancied secrets of Northanger Abbey, yet she is proved right, essentially if not circumstantially, in the ridiculous certitude, induced in her by a sudden immersion in 'culture', the impassioned surrender of her mind to sensational novels, that the ethos of the great house is not in fact what it appears to be, that its noble candour masks the base and shameful. Reality is more accessible to her absurdity than it is to the imperturbable good sense of her lover, the genially pedagogic Henry Tilney, the very type of the 'honest soul', the 'placid consciousness' *par excellence.*

But the judgements of *Mansfield Park* are not dialectical. They are uncompromisingly categorical. Alone among Jane Austen's novels, *Mansfield Park* is pledged to the single vision of the 'honest soul'. It knows that things are not what they will become but what an uncorrupted intelligence may perceive them to be from the first. Seven years after the publication of the *Phenomenology* this novel tells us in effect that Hegel is quite wrong in the method of judgement he propounds and exemplifies. It instructs us that the way to 'nobility' lies only through the explicit affirmation of this condition of being, not through its negation, that it lies through duty acknowledged and discharged, through a selfhood whose entelechy is bound up with the conditions of its present existence, through singleness of mind. 'Baseness' leads only to baseness. The negation of the self, far from being the means by which the self is realized, is its destruction—against Hegel's celebration of Rameau's great pandemic impersonation is set the degra׳ dation of the enchanting Henry Crawford whose striking histrionic talent is the fatal disposition of his being. 'Whether it were dignity, or pride, or tenderness, or re׳ morse, or whatever were to be expressed, he could do it with equal beauty. It was truly dramatic.' It is a mark of the weakness of his personal fabric that, although of large independent means, he toys with the thought of entering the Church or the Navy, the two professions by which Jane Austen set so much moral store—it is not as *callings* that he conceives them, only as opportunities for self׳ dramatization. His adultery with Maria Bertram is not only loveless but lustless; so far from being forgivable as passion, a free expression of selfhood, it is merely a role undertaken, a part played as the plot requires. Of Mary Crawford, whose charm almost equals her brother's, we are led to expect that her vivaciousness and audacity will constitute the beneficent counter׳principle to the stodginess which, as the novel freely grants, is one of the attributes of Mansfield Park. But in the outcome her wit is seen to be by no means an energy oᶜ Spirit pressing forward to new and freer and more developed modes of being. Actually its tendency is regressive—its depreciation of Mansfield Park is not an effort of liberation but an acquiescence in bondage, a cynical commitment to the way of the world, to the metropolitan society which Rousseau had denounced as the enemy of all true being.

For readers of our time *Mansfield Park* is likely to be a

distressing work. Even those who are of Jane Austen's party and absolute in their allegiance must make a special effort to come to terms with this novel. Those who are less fully pledged to its author are commonly alienated and angered by what they take to be its impercipient and restrictive moralism, its partisanship with duty and dullness, its crass respectability. It is not, however, the imputed philistinism of its particular moral judgements which con⁄stitutes the chief offence of *Mansfield Park*. This lies, rather, in the affront it offers to an essential disposition of the modern mind, a settled and cherished habit of perception and judgement—our commitment to the dialectical mode of apprehending reality is outraged by the militant cate⁄gorical certitude with which *Mansfield Park* discriminates between right and wrong. This disconcerts and discomfits us. It induces in us a species of anxiety. As how should it not? A work of art, notable for its complexity, devotes its energies, which we cannot doubt are of a very brilliant kind, to doing exactly the opposite of what we have learned to believe art ideally does and what we most love it for doing, which is to confirm the dialectical mode and mitigate the constraints of the categorical. *Mansfield Park* ruthlessly rejects the dialectical mode and seeks to impose the categorical constraints the more firmly upon us. It does not confirm our characteristic modern intuition that the enlightened and generous mind can discern right and wrong and good and bad only under the aspect of process and development, of futurity and the interplay and resolution of contradictions. It does not invite us to any of the pleasures which are to be derived from the transcendance of immediate and pragmatic judgement, such as grave, large⁄minded detachment, or irony, or confidence in the unfolding future. It is antipathetic to the temporality of the dialectical mode; the only moment of judgement it acknowledges is *now*: it is in the exigent present that things are what they really are, not in the unfolding future. A work of art informed by so claustral a view might well distress our minds, might well give rise to anxiety. And not least because we understand it to be saying that even the reality of the reader himself is not, as he might wish to think, what it may become, but ineluctably what it is now. This is a dark thought, an archaic thought, one that detaches us from the predilections of our culture. But when its first unease has been accommodated, it can be seen to have in it a curious power of comfort.

IV · THE HEROIC, THE BEAUTI-
FUL, THE AUTHENTIC

i

SOME YEARS AGO, IN WRITING ABOUT JANE
Austen, I drew upon an essay which Richard Simpson
contributed to the *North British Review* in 1870. It seemed
to me, as it still does, one of the best accounts of Jane
Austen's achievement that has ever been written. It is the
more remarkable in being perhaps the very first consideration of the subject undertaken in the spirit of serious
criticism—the first, that is, to go beyond mere expressions
of delight and regard, or calculations of the distance at
which Jane Austen stands from Walter Scott and Shakespeare, to address itself to a description of the novels in
their innerness and their largeness of import. As to the
latter, the essay takes for granted the full scope of the
novelist's concern, understanding that this does not reach
its limit at particular female destinies but extends to an
object no less general than 'man', to man in society and to
the complex process of his self-realization through society.
'Even as a unit,' Simpson says, 'man is only known to [Jane
Austen] in the process of his formation by social influences.
She broods over his history, not over his individual soul and
its secret workings, not over the analysis of its faculties and
organs. She sees him not as a solitary being completed in
himself, but only as completed in society.' And:'. . . She

contemplates virtues, not as fixed quantities or as definable qualities, but as . . . progressive states of mind. . . .'

This is admirable, and no less so is the perception that Jane Austen was, as the critic puts it, 'saturated' with a 'Platonic idea'—she was committed to the ideal of 'intelli⁄gent love', according to which the deepest and truest relationship that can exist between human beings is peda⁄gogic. This relationship consists in the giving and receiving of knowledge about right conduct, in the formation of one person's character by another, the acceptance of another's guidance in one's own growth. The idea of a love based in pedagogy may seem quaint to some modern readers and repellent to others, but unquestionably it plays a decisive part in the power and charm of Jane Austen's art. And if we attempt to explain the power and charm that the genre of the novel exercised in the nineteenth century, we must take full account of its pedagogic intention and of such love as a reader might feel was being directed towards him in the solicitude of the novel for *his* moral well⁄being, in its concern for the right course of his development.

Life seen under the aspect of instruction is scarcely a new vision in literature. In one degree or another, literature has always claimed such sanction as pedagogy affords. But it is especially salient in the Christian tradition and it asserts itself with a new energy when an accelerated social mobility makes right conduct problematical.

Yet despite the ascendancy of the pegagogic mode in the nineteenth century, the contemporary reader of educated tastes was not without some uneasiness about it. The sub⁄stance of this reservation is suggested by the admirable Victorian critic in his summary of Jane Austen's concep⁄tion of the moral life. At one point he falls into the language of warfare, speaks of 'struggles' and 'conquests', and says that 'the individual mind can only be represented by [Jane

Austen] as a battle-field where contending hosts are marshalled and where victory inclines now to one side and now to another'. This, we must feel, does not ring true; it does not accurately convey the nature of moral activity as Jane Austen conceives it. We have no difficulty in understanding why the critic resorts to the large military simile—it is a handy way of asserting that the novels are momentous in their significance, of claiming for them the respect that is traditionally given to works in the heroic mode, of which the military virtues are ultimately definitive, and most readily given to tragedy, the genre originally defined by its reliance upon the heroic mode. The critic, as we have seen, is beautifully aware of the large significances adumbrated by Jane Austen's novels, yet he is constrained to communicate the true state of the case in language not appropriate to it, to describe the pedagogic enterprise in terms borrowed from the anachronistic idiom of the heroic.

By its nature, pedagogy is at odds with the heroic genre of tragedy, to which it tacitly imputes a perverse self-indulgence, an arrogant disdain of reason, prudence, and morality. Tragedy, for its part, invites us to find in it some pedagogic purpose, but the invitation cannot really be thought to be made in good faith. We cannot convince ourselves that the two Oedipus tragedies teach us anything, or show the hero as learning anything. It is true that tragedies are often about knowing and not knowing, and they range themselves on the side of knowing. But this partisanship must be approached warily lest we find ourselves in the unhappy situation of those critics who tell us that Lear and Gloucester suffered to good purpose because their pain 'educated' them before they died. When, as with *Oedipus Rex*, a great tragedy is made to yield such conclusions as that fate is inscrutable and that it is a wise child who knows his own father, or, as with *King Lear*, that the

universe is uncomfortable and its governance morally in-
comprehensible, we decide that tragedy has indeed nothing
to do with the practical conduct of life except as it transcends and negates it, that it celebrates a mystery debarred
to reason, prudence, and morality. Which is why pedagogy
sets itself against tragedy—it imputes to tragedy an essential
lack of seriousness.

At a certain point in history the pedagogic literary mode
expressed its distrust of the heroic in an open antagonism.
Speaking of the genre of the novel, Jacques Barzun says
that 'from its beginnings in *Don Quixote* and *Tom Jones*
[it] has persistently made war on two things—our culture
and the heroic'. The novel, to be sure, did not fight alone:
the heroic mode found antagonists in its very citadel, the
theatre, as the juxtaposition of Falstaff and Hotspur or the
remorseless treatment of the heroic in *Troilus and Cressida*
will suggest. But Mr. Barzun is correct in fixing upon the
novel, the pedagogic genre *par excellence*, as the chief
opponent of the heroic view of life. Walter Benjamin speaks
of the impulse to impart instruction as a defining characteristic of story-telling and as a condition of its vitality.
Story-telling, he says, is oriented towards 'practical
interests'; it seeks to be 'useful'; it 'has counsel' to give;
the end it has in view is 'wisdom'. In so far as this is true,
the novel, which at least in its beginnings was committed
to story-telling, is of its nature opposed to the heroic.

What is, or was, the heroic? What is a hero?

A good answer was given by the late Robert Warshow
when, in an essay on Western films, he said: 'A hero is
one who looks like a hero.' Warshow was saying essentially
what Margarete Bieber had said in her book on the Greek
theatre, that the hero is an actor. The two statements,
especially Professor Bieber's, make it plain that the idea
of the hero is only secondarily a moral idea; to begin with,

it is no more so than the grace of a dancer is a moral idea. Nowadays our colloquial language makes the idea of the hero more or less coextensive with one of the moral qualities originally thought to be essential to it: 'hero' is our word for a man who commits an approved act of unusual courage. But in the ancient literary conception of the hero, courage is only a single element, and although it is essential, it is not in itself definitive. It is virtually taken for granted in a man who is favoured by the gods, as the hero is presumed to be, and who is even endowed with certain inherited traits of divinity. This favour or heritage of divinity makes itself fully apparent. The dignity it confers on the man is not latent, to be revealed or discerned eventually, but is wholly manifest in word and deed, in physique and comportment. It announces and demonstrates itself. The hero is one who looks like a hero; the hero is an actor—he acts out his own high sense of himself.

Not all cultures develop the idea of the heroic. I once had occasion to observe in connection with Wordsworth that in the Rabbinical literature there is no touch of the heroic idea. The Rabbis, in speaking of virtue, never mention the virtue of courage, which Aristotle regarded as basic to the heroic character. The indifference of the Rabbis to the idea of courage is the more remarkable in that they knew that many of their number would die for their faith. What is especially to our point is that, as ethical beings, the Rabbis never *see themselves*—it is as if the commandment which forbade the making of images extended to their way of conceiving the personal moral existence as well. They imagine no struggles, no dilemmas, no hard choices, no ironies, no destinies, nothing *interesting*; they have no thought of morality as drama. They would have been quite ready to understand the definition of the hero as an actor and to say that, as such, he was undeserving of the attention of serious men. Aristotle's virtuous man in his highest development quite precisely sees himself: he whose virtue is such that it wears the crowning perfection of *megalopsychia*, 'great-souledness' or 'aristocratic pride', is to be recognized by the way he comports himself, by his slow gait, his low-pitched voice, his measured diction, his conscious irony in dealing with inferiors—the virtuous man is an actor. And Hans Jonas, in his study of the Gnostic religion, comments on the theatrical element in the ethical system of the Stoics. ' "To play one's part"—that figure of speech on which Stoic ethics dwells so much—unwittingly reveals the fictitious element in the construction. A role played is substituted for a real function performed. The actors on the stage'—that is, the stage of the world on which the moral life is played—'behave "as if" they acted their choice, and "as if" their actions mattered. What actually matters is only to play well rather than badly, with no genuine relevance to the outcome. The actors, bravely playing, are their own audience.' This cosmic moral histrionism is at the furthest remove from the Rabbis. And if, in the Jewish tradition, we go back of the Rabbis to the Bible, we do not find the heroic there either. David, as a person, is of consummate interest to us, but the interest is not of the sort that attaches to heroes. Milton, in the Greek manner, does his best for Samson, but not even in Milton's poem, much less in Judges, is Samson really a hero. Oedipus confronting the mystery of human suffering is a hero; Job in the same confrontation is not.

The Greeks were under no illusion about the actuality of the hero. Aristotle makes this plain in his comparison of tragedy and comedy: it is only in the genre of tragedy that the hero exists, for tragedy shows men as better than they really are, which is to say, nobler, more impressive, more dignified. The whole import of tragedy depends upon

the 'elevation' of the hero, to which every external ele‑
ment of the drama—language, gesture, costume—must
contribute. There can be no comic hero, for comedy shows
men as worse than they really are, which is to say more
ignoble, less impressive, less dignified. We are puzzled to
know, when we meet the famous definitions for the first
time, why this philosopher, who thought of so much,
never thought of a literary genre which would show men as
they really are, neither better nor worse.

It is sometimes supposed that the comic is a response to
the tragic, that in its essence it is an adverse comment on
the heroic. But it is just as possible to say that the germ
of the heroic idea is to be found in the comic itself, that at
the moment at which men think of themselves as funny
they have conceived the idea of their dignity. As soon as
they joke about their natural functions, about the absurdity
of defecation and copulation and the oddness of the shapes
their bodies grow into, they are on the way to contriving
to appear nobler than they really are. How else do men
recognize their ignobility than by imagining their potential
nobility?—a state of being which in time will come to
burden and bore them and arouse their mockery.

In literature, as in our personal lives, the debate between
the heroic and the anti‑heroic principle would seem to be
a natural rhythm of the psyche, an alternation of commit‑
ment to the superego, which is the repository of our govern‑
ing ideals, and to the id, which is the locus of our instinctual
drives. In the Renaissance, however, the heroic style of the
superego was confronted with a new antagonism, that
which was offered by the ego, the aspect of the self which
has for its function the preservation of the self. The heroic
mode came under attack not only as being absurd in the
grandiose elevation of its style and in the moral pretensions
which this expressed, but also as standing in the way of the

practical conduct of life. The literary mind of the Renaissance was enchanted by the heroic idea and at the same
time profoundly critical of it. The ambivalence is memorial-
ized in the character and fate of Othello, whose defence-
lessness is a function of his conscious grandeur, of his
insensate commitment to the heroic style. This hero is
indeed an actor and his role is his doom.

Shakespeare's account of the career of Prince Hal exemplifies in a classic way the feeling of the Renaissance that
the heroic idea is an impediment to the practical management of life. If the young prince is to become a king he
must not only repudiate Falstaff, as from the first he intended, but also triumph over the captivating Harry
Hotspur, the very embodiment of the heroic ideal, praised
as such by Hal's own father: we are to understand that the
hedonist reprobate and the hero fixated in his role are at
one in infantile narcissism; both are in the service of an
anarchic principle. The transactions of Cervantes with the
concept of the heroic are too complex and paradoxical to
be specified here, but for our purpose it is enough to recall
of *Don Quixote* that it grew out of its author's simple intention of asserting the claims of quotidian practicality against
those of the heroic ideal. Fielding, the avowed and loving
disciple of Cervantes, was virtually obsessed by the discrepancy between the heroic tradition and the actual
world; he could think of no more delicious joke than to
bring the two together, the heroic and the actual, and
describe a brawl of village sluts in terms of a battle before
the walls of Troy, or to foist upon his readers in the status
of a hero a foundling whose name is not Oedipus but
Tom, which of all names he thought the most ridiculous.
To Fielding it was always an astonishing fact that literature as he knew it from his adoration of the Greek classics
was not consonant with life as he had to deal with it in

his magistrate's courtroom or in his sociological and criminological pamphlets. The literary mind of Europe increasingly inclined to join Swift in praise of the virtue of the man who makes two ears of corn or two blades of grass grow where only one grew before. The extent and fervour of its response to the claims of everyday life are attested to by Diderot's great *Encyclopédie*.

But the increasing concern with the actual, with the sub-stance of life in all its ordinariness and lack of elevation, was not directed to practicality alone. It also made the ground of a new, or rediscovered, kind of spiritual experi-ence. To emphasize the intractable material necessity of common life and what this implies of life's wonderlessness is to make all the more wonderful such moments of transcendence as may now and then occur. This, it will be recognized, is the basis of Joyce's conception of the 'epi-phany', literally a 'showing forth'. The assumption of the epiphany is that human existence is in largest part com-pounded of the dullness and triviality of its routine, devitalized or paralysed by habit and the weight of neces-sity, and that what is occasionally shown forth, although it is not divinity as the traditional Christian meaning of the word would propose, is nevertheless appropriate to the idea of divinity: it is what we call spirit. Often what is dis-closed is spirit in its very negation, as it has been diminished and immobilized by daily life. But there are times when the sudden disclosure transfigures the dull and ordinary, suffusing it with significance.[1] So far as Joyce thinks of the

---

[1] Richard Ellmann distinguishes between 'lyrical epiphanies' and 'bald, under-played epiphanies' (*James Joyce*, O.U.P., New York and London, 1959, p. 169). 'Sometimes the epiphanies are "eucharistic", another term arrogantly borrowed by Joyce from Christianity and invested with secular meaning. These are moments of fullness or of passion. Sometimes the epiphanies are rewarding for another reason, that they convey precisely the flavor of unpalatable experiences. The spirit, as Joyce characteristically held, manifested itself at both levels.' (p. 87)

epiphany as a genre in itself, he stays close to one of the
established implications of the word, that the revelation
takes place suddenly, in a flash. Yet we can perhaps con-
sider the whole of *Ulysses* as an epiphany, the continuous
showing forth of the spirit of Leopold Bloom out of the
intractable commonplaceness of his existence. This, of
course, is what makes the frequently remarked affinity of
Bloom with Don Quixote: in the existence of both men
the ordinary and actual are prepotent; both are in bondage
to daily necessity and to the manifest absurdity of their
bodies, and they thus stand at a polar distance from the
Aristotelean hero in the superbness of his aristocratic autonomy and dignity.[1] Yet both Bloom and Don Quixote
transcend the imposed actuality to become what we, by
some new definition of the word, are willing to call
heroes. The way down, as Heraclitus said, is the same thing
as the way up.

Between Joyce and Wordsworth the differences in personal temperament and public 'image' are wide indeed,
but we know from Joyce's letters that at a crucial moment
in his creative life, at the time of *Dubliners*, he held Wordsworth in unique esteem. It is Wordsworth, Joyce writes,
who 'of all English men of letters best deserves [the] word
"genius" '. We cannot be far wrong if we take it that a
chief ground for this superlative judgement was Wordsworth's devotion to the epiphany.

The Wordsworthian epiphany has two distinct though
related forms. In one, spirit shows forth from Nature; the
sudden revelation communicates to the poet a transcendent
message which bears upon the comprehension of human

---

[1] In saying this, I accept the common view of Bloom as a short, pudgy
man. But in fact he is neither short nor fat. His height is 5ft. 9½in., which
would make him rather taller than average in the Dublin of 1904. And at that
height his 164 pounds do not, at his age, make him overweight.

existence or upon the direction his own life should take. An example of this kind of epiphany is Wordsworth's experience of the mountain dawn which dedicates him to the priesthood of the imagination. The other, less grandiose and more closely connected with Joyce's epiphanies,[1] has as its locus and agent some unlikely person—a leech-gatherer, a bereft and deserted woman, an old man on the road—who, without intention, by something said or done, or not done, suddenly manifests the quality of his own particular being and thus implies the wonder of being in general. Lowness of social station, lowness even in a biological sense, is a necessary condition of the persons who provide Wordsworth's epiphanies: a man so old that he can scarcely move, a woman stupefied by despair, an idiot boy who says 'Burr, burr, burr' and has no name for the moon. We wonder, indeed, whether people as marginal to developed life as these can be thought to partake of full humanity; yet this is of course why Wordsworth has chosen them, for what the epiphanies disclose is that these persons forcibly exist as human beings. In this context the stress properly falls not on the word 'human' but on 'beings'. It is impossible to exaggerate the force that the word 'be' has for Wordsworth. He uses it as if with the consciousness that it makes the name of God. When he undertakes to argue his sister-in-law into a correct appreciation of 'Resolution and Independence', he says, 'What is brought forward? "A lonely place, a Pond, by which an old man *was*, far from all house or home"—not stood, not sat, but "was"—the figure represented in the most naked simplicity possible.'[2]

[1] Among which, however, we must include the moment of glory on the strand when the world shows forth its beauty to Stephen Dedalus and, as for Wordsworth, makes the occasion of his dedication as a priest of art.

[2] Wordsworth quotes (letter of 14 June 1802) from an early draft of the poem, now lost.

Nowadays in the critical consideration of Wordsworth
the name of Rousseau appears less frequently than it did
earlier in the century. Doubtless this revision in our esti-
mate of Rousseau's influence on Wordsworth is justified,
but there is one point of connection between the two men
that requires to be kept in mind—the passionate emphasis
each of them put upon the individual's experience of his
existence. Rousseau calls this, as we have seen, the 'sentiment of being'. Wordsworth calls it by the same name.
For both men the sentiment of being was an unassailable
intuition. It figured in their minds as it did in the mind of
Walt Whitman, who said that it is 'the hardest basic fact
and only entrance to all facts'. The facts to which this fact
is entrance are those of the social and political life—it is
through our conscious certitude of our personal selfhood
that we reach our knowledge of others.

ii

The idea of sincerity can of course never be far from our
thoughts when we speak of either Rousseau or Wordsworth. It does not, however, bear upon their ontological
concern, their preoccupation with the sentiment of being,
or at least it does not do so in the first instance. I remarked
earlier that it would be only absurd to say of the patriarch
Abraham that he was or was not a sincere man. It would
be similarly absurd to undertake an assessment of the
sincerity of the protagonist of Wordsworth's poem
Michael, who, like Abraham, was a shepherd, a father, and
very old. The poem comes to its climax in a single line
which no one who has read it ever forgets: when Michael,
after having lost his son Luke to the corruption of the city,
continues to build the sheepfold which he and the boy
had ceremonially begun together, his neighbours report of

him that sometimes he sat the whole day 'And never lifted up a single stone'. It would go beyond absurdity, it would be a kind of indecency, to raise the question of the sincerity of this grief even in order to affirm it. Indeed, the impossibility of our raising such a question is of the essence of our experience of the poem. Michael says nothing; he *expresses* nothing. It is not the case with him as it is with Hamlet that he has 'that within which passeth show'. There is no within and without: he and his grief are one. We may not, then, speak of sincerity. But our sense of Michael's being, of—so to speak—his being-in-grief, comes to us as a surprise, as if it were exceptional in its actuality, and valuable. And we are impelled to use some word which denotes the nature of this being and which accounts for the high value we put upon it. The word we employ for this purpose is 'authenticity'.

It is a word of ominous import. As we use it in reference to human existence, its provenance is the museum, where persons expert in such matters test whether objects of art are what they appear to be or are claimed to be, and therefore worth the price that is asked for them—or, if this has already been paid, worth the admiration they are being given. That the word has become part of the moral slang of our day points to the peculiar nature of our fallen condition, our anxiety over the credibility of existence and of individual existences. An eighteenth-century aesthetician states our concern succinctly—'Born Originals,' Edward Young said, 'how comes it to pass that we die Copies?'

No one has much difficulty with the answer to this question. From Rousseau we learned that what destroys our authenticity is society—our sentiment of being depends upon the opinion of other people. The ideal of authentic personal being stands at the very centre of Rousseau's thought. Yet I think that its presence there, however forcible it may have seemed to Rousseau's contemporaries, is rather too abstract, or too moderate, to command the modern imagination. The authenticity which the *First Discourse* ascribes to pre-social man seems to us to consist in his merely being not inauthentic; the authenticity which Rousseau ascribes to the bourgeois republican of Geneva is defined by his not being a Parisian, or, at its most vivid, by his having a week-end cottage, a gun, and some friends to drink and shoot with. Nowadays our sense of what authenticity means involves a degree of rough concreteness or of extremity which Rousseau, with his abiding commit-ment to an ideal of patrician civility, does not give us but which Wordsworth pre-eminently does. Michael is as actual, as hard, dense, weighty, perdurable as any stone he lifts up or lets lie.

To one of Wordsworth's epiphanies of authentic being Coleridge took strong exception—'The Idiot Boy', he said, is inevitably offensive to the sensibilities of the reader. This is an opinion with which we are at present less in agreement than we might once have been; yet the poem still provokes resistance in us. But when we admire it, as we should, we cannot fail to see that its offensiveness is part of its intention. That this is so suggests that authenticity is implicitly a polemical concept, fulfilling its nature by dealing aggressively with received and habitual opinion, aesthetic opinion in the first instance, social and political opinion in the next. One topic of its polemic, which has reference to both aesthetic and social opinion, is the error of the view that beauty is the highest quality to which art may aspire.

Something can be learned about the ideal of authenticity in its relation to beauty by calling to mind the artistic quality that is—or was—known as the sublime. The sublime and the authentic are certainly not equivalent, but they have one trait in common, a settled antagonism to beauty. When Edmund Burke undertakes his *Philosophical Enquiry into the Origin of our Ideas of the Sublime and Beautiful*, he is perfectly forthright about the social import of the opposition he sets up between the two qualities that high art may have. This brilliant young man from the provinces with a career to make and the firmest intention of making it leaves us in no doubt that his aesthetic preference, his choice of the sublime as against the beautiful, is dictated by his sense of how society is constituted and of how it may be dominated and made to serve his purpose, and by his commitment to the energies of his genius. He explicitly connects the sublime with masculinity, with manly *ambition*; the defining characteristic of the sublime, he tells us, is its capacity for arousing the emotion of 'terror', which calls forth in us the power to meet and master it; the experience of terror stimulates an energy of aggression and dominance. Beauty, on the contrary, is to be associated with femininity. It seduces men to inglorious indolence and ignoble hedonism. Burke's account of what happens to the masculine organism under the deleterious influence of beauty makes what is perhaps the only funny passage in the long canon of aesthetic theory. Beauty, it tells us, is that quality of an object which excites love; it acts 'by relaxing the solids of the whole system' of the viewer, to this effect: 'The head reclines something on one side; the eyelids are more closed than usual, and the eyes roll gently with an inclination to the object, the mouth is a little opened, and the breath drawn slowly, with now and then a low sigh: the whole body is composed, and the hands fall idly to the sides. All this is accompanied with an inward sense of melting and languor.'

Burke's denigration of beauty in favour of the energy called forth by the sublime put its mark on much of the aesthetic theory of the following age. Schiller, for example, under the influence of the *Philosophical Enquiry*, proposed that beauty has two modes: one is 'melting beauty', which relaxes our physical and moral nature, the other is 'energiz⁄ing beauty', which, by confronting us with difficult, harsh, and even disagreeable experiences, increases our 'elasticity and power of prompt action'. Both modes of beauty, he tells us, aid in the development of man, the usefulness of each of them depending upon the condition of culture at a given time. Schiller, writing his *Aesthetic Letters* between 1793 and 1801, inclined to the view that energy was the order of the day. 'The man who lives under the indulgent sway of taste is in need of energizing beauty; he is only too ready, once he has reached a state of sophisticated refine⁄ment, to trifle away the strength he brought with him from the state of savagery.'

We are once more reminded of the part played by Rousseau in the aesthetic revolution of the later eighteenth century. Burke is the legendary antagonist of Rousseau, Schiller his disciple, but both men are responding to his denunciation of the arts for their intention of *pleasing*. It was this, we have seen, that made the arts, for Rousseau, the paradigm of society in its characteristic deterioration of the sentiment of being. When Burke says, 'I call Beauty a social quality', he means pretty much what Rousseau meant when he said that the arts have the effect of socializ⁄ing men, which is to say, of making them passive and acquiescent. But where both Burke and Schiller part com⁄pany with Rousseau is in perceiving that the arts can have an intention and effect other than that of pleasing, that they can serve some other purpose than that of indulging their audience.

Here we should perhaps take note of a slight semantic complication. One connotation of the word 'please' tends to limit its use to objects which are relatively small either in size or import, those to which 'taste' can appropriately be applied; Burke specifically makes smallness an attribute of beauty. Another connotation of 'please' suggests the idea of social ingratiation. But the word 'pleasure' can repel these ignoble meanings and suggest others of greater dignity, doubtless because of its habitual association with the word 'pain' and also because of the actual interfusion of pleasure and pain (a matter to which Burke gives considerable attention); as a consequence, pleasure persists for a long time in aesthetic theory as the proper end of art. The sub/ lime does not please; but it does give pleasure, at least so far as pleasure is synonymous with gratification: it produces, Burke says, 'a sort of swelling and triumph that is extremely grateful to the human mind'. Not until our own time will critics give up trying to justify art by the pleasure it gives and even be willing to say, as Susan Sontag does, that pleasure has nothing to do with the artistic experience.[1] This view, which takes us a little but not wholly aback, has had its ground prepared by two centuries of aesthetic theory and artistic practice which have been less and less willing to take account of the habitual preferences of the audience. The artist—as he comes to be called—ceases to be the craftsman or the performer, dependent upon the approval of the audience. His reference is to himself only, or to some transcendent power which—or who—has de/ creed his enterprise and alone is worthy to judge it.

We rightly speak of this change as a revolution. And, having done so, it seems natural to connect it with social revolution: down goes the audience, up comes the artist:

[1] Miss Sontag limits her disjunction of pleasure and the artistic experience to her view of a proper response to works of our present period (*Against Interpretation*, New York, 1966; London, 1967, pp. 302–3). My essay 'The Fate of Pleasure' (*Beyond Culture*, New York and London, 1965) deals with the present status of pleasure in relation to art.

'*A bas, les lecteurs—à la lanterne!*' But actually the situation is considerably more complex than that. In *The Mirror and the Lamp*, his admirable account of the aesthetic revolution, M. H. Abrams speaks of the fate of the audience as being a 'drastic' one, and so it is. But this fate does not consist simply in the loss of its old status and privileges; something is gained as well as lost—something is gained *through* the loss. The fate is as paradoxical as it is drastic: if down goes the audience it is a Fortunate Fall that it takes; the loss of its Eden of gratified desire brings with it covenants of redemption and the offer of a higher, more significant life. Certainly the modern audience does not seem to regret having had to exchange indulgence and flattery for the exigencies of its new relation to art. On the contrary, the devotion now given to art is probably more fervent than ever before in the history of culture. This devotion takes the form of an extreme demand: now that art is no longer required to please, it is expected to provide the spiritual substance of life. As for the artist, even while he asserts his perfect autonomy and regards his audience with indiffer-ence, or with hostility and contempt, he is sustained by the certitude that he alone can provide what the audience most deeply needs.[1]

---

[1] I am aware that this description of the relation of the audience to the art of its own day is anachronistic. It applies to the audience and art of the period which is now called 'Modern' by the historians of culture and under-stood by them to be in the past and succeeded by a period which they call 'Post-Modern'. At the present moment, art cannot be said to make exigent demands upon the audience. That segment of our culture which is at all re-sponsive to contemporary art is wholly permeable by it. The situation no longer obtains in which the experience of a contemporary work begins in resistance and proceeds by relatively slow stages to a comprehending or submissive ad-miration. The artist now can make scarcely anything which will prove really exigent to the audience, which will outrage its habitual sensibility. The audience likes or does not like, is pleased or not pleased—the faculty of 'taste' has re-established itself at the centre of the experience of art.

An initial difficulty arises because the audience is not readily conscious of what it wants of the artist and of how much it has come to rely upon him. Yet in the end there is no failure of communication. What the audience demands of the artist—really demands, in its unconscious desire—and what the artist thinks it ought to be given turn out to be the same thing. We know, of course, what that is: it is the senti' ment of being. A synonym for the sentiment of being is that 'strength' which, Schiller tells us, 'man brought with him from the state of savagery' and which he finds it so difficult to preserve in a highly developed culture. The sentiment of being is the sentiment of being strong. Which is not to say powerful: Rousseau, Schiller, and Wordsworth are not concerned with energy directed outward upon the world in aggression and dominance, but, rather, with such energy as contrives that the centre shall hold, that the circumference of the self keep unbroken, that the person be an integer, impenetrable, perdurable, and autonomous in being if not in action.[1]

And through the nineteenth century art has as one of its chief intentions to induce in the audience the sentiment of being, to recruit the primitive strength that a highly de' veloped culture has diminished. To this end it proposes a variety of spiritual exercises, among which are suffering and despair and cosmic defiance; conscious sympathy with the being of others; comprehension of the processes of society; social alienation. As the century advances the sentiment of being, of being strong, is increasingly sub' sumed under the conception of personal authenticity. The work of art is itself authentic by reason of its entire self' definition: it is understood to exist wholly by the laws of its own being, which include the right to embody painful,

[1] Here, of course, Schiller differs from Burke, who, as we have seen, set store by the 'ambition' to which art, in the mode he most admired, gives rise.

ignoble, or socially inacceptable subject-matters. Similarly
the artist seeks his personal authenticity in his entire autono-
mousness—his goal is to be as self-defining as the art-object
he creates. As for the audience, its expectation is that
through its communication with the work of art, which
may be resistant, unpleasant, even hostile, it acquires the
authenticity of which the object itself is the model and the
artist the personal example. When, in Sartre's *La Nausée*,
the protagonist Roquentin, at the end of his diary of queasy
despair, permits himself to entertain a single hope, it is that
he may write a story which will be 'beautiful and hard as
steel and make people ashamed of their existence'. The
authentic work of art instructs us in our inauthenticity and
adjures us to overcome it.

Sartre's admired younger colleague Nathalie Sarraute
observes in her essay on Flaubert that the quality which
'today we call "inauthenticity" ' and with which everyone
is on such familiar terms was once 'a new psychic sub-
stance'; we owe its discovery to Flaubert, who 'unearthed'
or 're-created' it in *Madame Bovary*. It is this quality which
wholly characterizes the protagonist of the novel. 'We all
remember', Mme Sarraute says, 'that *trompe l'oeil* universe,
the world seen through the eyes of Madame Bovary: her
desires, her imaginings, the dreams on which she seeks
to build her existence, all of which are made up of a succession of cheap images drawn from the most debased, discredited forms of romanticism. One has only to recall her
adolescent day-dreams, her marriage, her love of luxury,
her vision of the lives lived by the "upper crust", of
"artistic and Bohemian circles" of Parisian life, all roles
that she was continually playing for others and for herself
and which were based on the most platitudinous of conventions.'

This, of course, says nothing new about Madame Bovary;

it is the accepted thing to say about her. I believe that it is not wholly accurate and that this poor doomed Emma, although inauthenticity certainly does touch her, is not a being of no actuality or worth whatever. She is not, it can be granted, a person of the finest development, but her endowment is not to be despised. She has a degree of courage, although of an imprudent sort, an attractive presence, a sexuality which is urgent when once it is aroused, an imagination which kindles to the idea of experience and envisions a society in which people are interesting and valued, and a will to overcome the nullity of her existence and to make, or seize, what is called a life. Doubtless something is lacking in her temperament, but not everything, and not enough to justify the condescension with which most readers think they ought to regard her. But I quote Mme Sarraute's version of the received view because its relentlessly censorious tone suggests the moral intensity we now direct upon questions of authenticity. The unhappy Emma Bovary was authentic at least in being unhappy to the point of distraction and in the peculiar horror of her death, but such inauthenticity as is rightly to be attributed to her makes it impossible for Mme Sarraute to give the forlorn creature even a wry compassion. A similar harshness of judgement informs Mme Sarraute's fiction, beginning with her first book, *Tropismes*, a work which induces us to wonder why this gifted and imperious author should choose as the objects of her fierce discernment such *little* and, so to speak, merely incidental persons as she depicts, whose existences, as minuscule as they are inauthentic, need not, we might suppose, impinge upon hers in any significant way. Why does she descend from the height of her privileged state of being to make explicit her disgust at the nothingness of these persons who, as the title of the work proposes, are not persons at all?

The answer is to be found in the famous sentence with which Sartre concludes his vision of the modern damnation, *Huis Clos*: 'Hell is other people.' This maxim is uttered by a detestable selfdeceiver and it is by no means the one that the play would enforce, which is, rather, the Miltonic 'Myself am Hell'. But it makes the significant modern qualification of the older primary truth—it proposes the infernal outcome of the modern social existence as Rousseau described and deplored it, in which the sentiment of individual being depends upon other people. All other people, the whole community up and down the scale of sentience and of cultural development, make the Hell of recognized and experienced inauthenticity. They make the inhabited nothingness of the modern world. They speak to us of our own condition; we are members one of another. Certain exemptions are made: the poor, the oppressed, the violent, the primitive. But whoever occupies a place in the social order in which we ourselves are situated is known to share the doom. It does not matter how small the place is, just so it be tenable: when Sartre undertakes to examine an example of inauthentic being, he chooses a person as little and as merely incidental as any of the subjects of *Tropismes*—that notorious waiter of his who sees himself not as a human being but as a waiter and finds his fulfillment in acting out his assigned role. 'We are all ill', Freud said. No less are we all inauthentic.

It isn't, then, hardness of heart that makes Mme Sarraute speak of Emma Bovary with harsh contempt; it is fear— the terror, as Sartre defines it in an essay on Mme Sarraute, of the Hell of dehumanization that inauthenticity is. She has, Sartre says, 'a protoplasmic vision of our interior universe: roll away the stone of the commonplace and we find discharges, slobberings, mucus; hesitant amoebalike movements.' By the word 'commonplace'—'this excellent word'

—Sartre means to designate 'our most hackneyed thoughts, inasmuch as these thoughts have become the meeting-place of the community'. And he goes on: 'It is here that each of us finds himself as well as the others. The common-place belongs to everybody and it belongs to me; in me, it belongs to everybody; it is the presence of everybody in me. In its very essence it is generality; in order to appropriate it, an act is necessary, an act through which I shed my particularity in order to adhere to the general, in order to become generality. Not at all like everybody, but, to be exact, the incarnation of everybody.' This is Hell, and no aspect of it so cruel as the devices of illusion by which it frustrates our efforts to extricate ourselves from the generality of the commonplace and to stand forth in the authenticity of particular being. If Madame Bovary receives less com-passion than her fate claims, if we put ourselves at a distance from her, by condescension as many do, by harsh con-tempt as Mme Sarraute does, it is because some attitude must be devised which controls the fear which arises in us at the fate of this poor damned soul who, seeking to escape the Hell that was the commonplace of Yonville, enters the Hell that was the commonplace of the high culture of her nation. If we do not put the distance of condescension or contempt between us and her, we shall have to know that when Flaubert said, '*Madame Bovary—c'est moi*', he was not making a preposterous paradox. We shall have to under-stand that Madame Bovary is each one of us.

'Points have we all of us within our souls / Where all stand single.' Wordsworth said this in 1805 and the passage of time has not, it would seem, diminished the powerful charm of these points of singleness. But how are they to be reached? Mme Sarraute, although she is very grand in what she says about the naïve purposes of the genre of the novel in the age before our own, does not liberate herself—does not wish to—from the pedagogic function that the novel traditionally discharged. No less than Jane Austen she is concerned to teach her readers how they are not to be if they really wish to *be*. It is easy at least to understand how not to be: we must not be like anyone else. But how does one actually proceed to this end? Our spirits fail when we are told by Mme Sarraute that, with the single exception of *Madame Bovary*, Flaubert himself is inauthentic in all his novels. But at least the artist can, on some occasions, evade the general Hell. He does so, Mme Sarraute says, by his intransigent subjectivity, 'purged of all impurities' of convention and tradition, by refusing the commonplaces that the culture treacherously provides for his convenience and comfort. We of the audience, however, are in less fortunate case.

According to Mme Sarraute, the inauthenticity of Emma Bovary consists in her using as the stuff of her dreams the 'cheap images drawn from the most debased, discredited forms of romanticism'. Would Madame Bovary, we wonder, have lived a more authentic life, would her sentiment of being have more nearly approached singleness and particularity, if at the behest of a more exigent taste she had chosen as the stuff of her dreams the well-made, expensive images of a more creditable form of romanticism? Will not any art—the most certifiedly authentic, the most shaming— provide sustenance for the inauthenticity of those who consciously shape their experience by it? It was the peculiar inauthenticity which comes from basing a life on the very best cultural objects that Nietzsche had in mind when he coined the terrible phrase, 'culture-Philistine'. What he means by this is the inversion of the bourgeois resistance to art which we usually call Philistinism; he means the use of the art and thought of high culture, of the highest culture, for purposes of moral accreditation, which in our time announces itself in the facile acceptance of the shame that art imputes and in the registration of oneself in the company of those who, because they see themselves as damned, are saved.

Rousseau is not mocked. The arts no longer seek to 'please', but pleasing was never the only technique of seduction, and art can still lead us into making the sentiment of our being dependent upon the opinion of others The concerted effort of a culture or of a segment of a culture to achieve authenticity generates its own conventions, its generalities, its commonplaces, its maxims, what Sartre, taking the word from Heidegger, calls the 'gabble'. To the gabble Sartre has himself by now made his contribution. As has Mme Sarraute; as did Gide; as did Lawrence—as must anyone who undertakes to satisfy our modern demand for reminders of our fallen state and for reasons why we are to be ashamed of our lives.

V · SOCIETY AND AUTHENTICITY

i

WHAT I TAKE TO BE THE PARADIGMATIC literary expression of the modern concern with authenticity is Joseph Conrad's great short novel *Heart of Darkness*, which appeared, with some appropriateness, in the next to the last year of the nineteenth century. This troubling work has no manifest polemical intention but it contains in sum the whole of the radical critique of European civilization that has been made by literature in the years since its publication.

In several respects the story has a striking affinity with Diderot's *Neveu de Rameau*. A man of unimpeachable moral character, a sensitive and reflective man but not inclined to raise radical questions about life, in short, an 'honest soul', a Diderot-*Moi*, is brought into confrontation with a *Lui*, who, however, is not a wild genius of cynicism like Diderot's Rameau but a man whose foul and bloody deeds make him what the terms of the story permit us to call a devil. Yet Marlow, the 'honest soul' who narrates the story, accords Kurtz an admiration and loyalty which amount to homage, and not, it would seem, in spite of his deeds but because of them.

As with Diderot's Rameau, it is scarcely possible to describe the character of Kurtz at once summarily and accurately. It is of the essence of his fate that Kurtz is implicated in one of the most brazen political insincerities ever perpetrated. The Berlin Congress, convened by Bismarck in 1885, established the King of the Belgians, Leopold II, in personal possession of and sovereignty over the so-called Congo Free State. Leopold's rule, through his surrogates, was absolute and ruthless, carried out with monstrous cruelty, but the royal Tartuffe had no difficulty in convincing the world that he was doing the work of civilization, bringing light to the brothers who sat in darkness. Marlow has no sooner set foot in the Congo than he perceives and is revolted by the discrepancy between these avowals of beneficent purpose and the terrible actuality of heartless oppression. But Kurtz, who is an agent of one of the great Belgian trading companies, at least for a time carries on his work in the belief that he is opening the country not only to trade but to the light that shines from Europe, and there is no clear indication in the story that he ever recognizes, let alone repudiates, the vast hypocrisy his nation is practising.

To the making of Kurtz, we are told, all Europe has contributed: the nationality of his parents is mixed; he is an amateur, more or less gifted, of the high arts, a writer, a painter, a musician; he professes the rational altruistic ethic of educated Europeans of good will. Marlow first hears of him as a man of superior intellectual and moral qualities which isolate him from his colleagues and make him the object of their envy and spite. The stunning *peripeteia* of the story is the revelation that Kurtz, having gone alone to collect ivory far up the Congo River, has become the chief and virtually the god of a local tribe, his rule being remarkable for its cruelty.

Kurtz, it must be clear, did not choose the life of savagery out of any sentimental illusion that it is noble and virtuous. On the contrary, he is appalled by it—one of his high-minded reports on the natives which Marlow reads after his death breaks off suddenly with the scrawl, 'Exterminate all the brutes!' And Marlow himself, although on one occasion he feels the frightening fascination of the savage life, allows it none of the charm that anthropologists commonly discover in tribal ways; he cannot withhold admiration from the manly grace of the natives but he looks upon the culture that bred them as sordid and terrible, in its own fashion as evil as the European culture which oppresses it. His word for it is Biblical and conclusive: it is the 'abomination'. Nor does Marlow suggest that Kurtz, by embracing savagery, has found redemption in any personal moral sense: he has purged himself of none of the European vices, not even greed. For Marlow, nevertheless, Kurtz is a hero of the spirit whom he cherishes as Theseus at Colonus cherished Oedipus: he sinned for all mankind. By his regression to savagery Kurtz had reached as far down beneath the constructs of civilization as it was possible to go, to the irreducible truth of man, the innermost core of his nature, his heart of darkness. From that Stygian authenticity comes illumination, the light cast not only on the souls of the Belgian business agents, servants of what Marlow calls a 'flabby, pretending, weak-eyed devil', but also on the soul of Kurtz's dedicated fiancée, who embodies all the self-cherishing, self-deceiving idealism of Europe, that noble 'Intended', monumental in her bereavement, appalling to Marlow in her certitude that her lost lover had been the reproachless knight of altruism.

But if, by this light, Marlow sees civilization as fraudulent and shameful, we yet confront the paradox that at the same time he has a passionate commitment to civilization, just so it is the right sort. Which is to say, just so it is English. The brilliant scene with which the story opens is set on a cruising yawl in the estuary of the Thames and is in effect a hymn, in which Marlow and the primary narrator join their voices, to the Englishness of the river. The aspect it would have had for the colonizing Romans is conjured up—no less primordially dark, inscrutable, threatening than the Congo seems to nineteenth-century Europeans. With the passing of the centuries, however, the English river has become an object of veneration for good men, who see it 'in the august light of abiding memories'. And the Thames has its own light, it is a source of light to the world: 'Light came from this river.' The great adventurers and settlers have sailed out from it—Marlow speaks of them as 'bearers of a spark from the sacred fire'. They carried to distant lands 'the seeds of commonwealth', and, not least of England's beneficences, 'the germ of empire'. To be sure, adventurers had set out from other lands too; we are to hear, later in the story, of the French, the Germans, and of course much of the Belgians. But they were wholly unlike the English. 'These chaps were not much account really', says Marlow. 'They were con-querors, and for that you want only brute force. . . . They grabbed what they could for the sake of what was in it. . . . It was just robbery with violence. . . .' And he goes on: 'The conquest of the earth, which mostly means the taking it away from those who have a different complexion or slightly flatter noses than ourselves, is not a pretty thing when you look at it too much. What redeems it is the idea only. An idea at the back of it; not a sentimental pretence but an idea; and an unselfish belief in the idea—something you can set up, and bow down before, and offer a sacrifice to.' Marlow does not doubt that it is the English alone who have such an idea.

Heart of Darkness, then, is a story that strangely moves in two quite opposite directions—on the one hand, to the view that civilization is of its nature so inauthentic that personal integrity can be wrested from it only by the in-version of all its avowed principles; on the other hand, to the categorical assertion that civilization can and does fulfil its announced purposes, not universally, indeed, but at least in the significant instance of one particular nation.

Today it is scarcely possible to read Marlow's celebration of England without irony; to many, especially among the English themselves, it is bound to seem patently absurd. The present state of opinion does not countenance the making of discriminations among imperialisms, present or past, and the idea that more virtue might be claimed for one nation than another is given scant credence. But this was not always the case. Having the choice to make, Conrad himself elected to become English exactly because he believed England to be a *good* nation. Nor was the judgement idiosyncratic to Conrad; it was shared by many who were not themselves English.[1]

Indeed, in the nineteenth century there was widespread belief that England produced a moral type which made it unique among nations. The opinion was given notable literary expression by Alfred de Vigny in his story about the young French officer who learned political virtue as the prisoner-of-war of Admiral Collingwood; by Herman Melville in the creation of Captain Vere; and by Gobineau in the character of the large-souled English admiral who finds his fulfilment in the solitude of a Greek island. This moral type which England was thought uniquely to have produced had as its chief qualities probity and candour. That, in the three instances I have adduced, the moral type should be discovered in officers of the Navy is scarcely

---

[1] Freud was among them. In a letter of 1939 to H. G. Wells, he says (the letter is written in English), '... Since I first came to England as a boy of eighteen years, it became an intense wish phantasy of mine to settle in this country and become an Englishman.'

fortuitous, for the English themselves gave the seafaring profession a special place in their imagination of the moral life, not surprising in an island people. The sailing officer was admired as the exemplar of a professional code which prescribed an uncompromising commitment to duty, a con/ tinuous concentration of the personal energies upon some impersonal end, the subordination of the self to some general good. It was the officer's response to the imperatives of this code that made for the singleness of mind and the open/ ness of soul imputed to him. Not least among the traits which inspired respect was his ability to meet the practical demands of an exigent trade, his technical competence painfully acquired through an apprenticeship which began in his boyhood. Gentleman though he was, he *worked*. And at the close of the century Conrad's Marlow speaks of work, which he also calls 'efficiency', as the great device— by implication peculiarly English—for getting through life with fortitude and dignity, the only protection against the despair which threatens when we permit ourselves to con/ template the nature of our existence. Work is the sure means of keeping oneself sound and whole, worthy of one's own respect, true to one's own self.

Marlow's tone as he says this is oddly not a good one. It is jaunty and glib, as if out of embarrassment—by 1899 the work/ethic, as we now familiarly call it, was a little fatigued. It had not, however, lost all the great power it exercised over the English mind through the century. In the national life the idea of the task, dutifully undertaken and cheerfully carried forward, figured as the principle of civilization itself. In the personal life it was the principle which guaranteed the trait on which the English most prided themselves, their sincerity, by which they meant their single/minded relation to things, to each other, and to themselves.

Emerson had no doubt that sincerity was the defining quality of the English character. In his *English Traits*, published in 1856, he recurs to it frequently and with vivacious admiration. Sincerity, he says, is the basis of the English national moral style. 'We will not have to do with a man in a mask,' he conceives the English to be saying. 'Let us know the truth. Draw a straight line, hit whom and where it will.' The English, Emerson tells us, are blunt in expressing what they think and they expect others to be no less so; their confidence in each other makes them unique among nations: 'English believes in English. The French feel the moral superiority of this probity.' And Emerson goes on to say that the superiority is not merely moral; the practical power of the English 'rests on their national sincerity'.

His happy surprise over the sincerity of the English makes us wonder what Emerson could have been used to in his native land, what sinister subtleties of dissimulation had been practised upon him in Concord, Massachusetts. Henry James is not exactly simple on the subject of any‚ thing that has to do with Americans, but the general tendency of his work would seem to confirm the opinion which once prevailed—how curious it now seems!—that Americans, being wholly innocent, were wholly sincere, that American sincerity was as certified as that of children, peasants, and nineteenth‚century dogs. Actually, of course, Emerson's surprise at the sincerity of the English does not imply that he thought his countrymen were deficient in the trait in the sense that they were given over to duplicity. The difference between the English and Americans that Emer‚ son was responding to was not the same as the difference between the English and the French; its nature is suggested by what Tocqueville observed of the tendency of American speech to be elaborate and abstract. Tocqueville did not suggest that Americans were being insincere in talking so. They were hiding nothing, they talked as they did because they lived in a democracy. The democratic dispensation required them to shape their speech not by the standards of a particular class or circle but by their sense of the opinion of the public, and it is this, Tocqueville says, which makes their mode of expression abstract rather than concrete, general rather than specific, periphrastic rather than direct.[1] The democratic style doesn't signify an absence of sincerity; it does, however, indicate that the personal self to which the American would wish to be true is not the private, solid, intractable self of the Englishman.

And in this respect the American self can be taken to be a microcosm of American society, which has notably lacked the solidity and intractability of English society; it is little likely to be felt by its members as being palpably *there*. The testimony on this score is one of the classic elements of nineteenth-century American cultural history. James Fenimore Cooper, Hawthorne, Henry James, all in one way or another said that American society was, in James's phrase, 'thinly composed', lacking the thick, coarse actuality which the novelist, as he existed in their day, needed for the practice of his craft. It did not offer him the palpable material, the *stuff*, out of which novels were made. What came as a revelation to American visitors to England was exactly the impermeability of English society, the solidness of the composition, the thick, indubitable *thereness* which enforced upon its members a

[1] That the mode of speech Tocqueville found characteristically American still persists is suggested by a snatch of conversation which was heard on the B.B.C. in 1969, between the Queen and the then new American Ambassador to Britain. In the course of a call being paid by the Ambassador, the Queen inquired whether he was by now settled and comfortable in his house, to which he replied: 'We are still, in the residence, subject to some discomfiture and inconvenience owing to certain elements of refurbishment.'

sort of primary sincerity—the free acknowledgement that in one respect, at least, they were *not* free, that their exist-ences were bound by their society, determined by its particularities. About their being social rather than tran-scendent beings the English told the truth to themselves and the world. It is most engaging in Emerson that he should have taken so lively a pleasure in the moral style that followed from this avowal, for the characteristic tendency of his thought is to deny what the English affirm.[1]

The Hegelian terms which I touched on earlier bear upon the difference between the two nations. Americans, we might say—D. H. Lawrence did in effect say it fifty years ago—had moved into that historical stage of Spirit which produces the 'disintegrated' or 'alienated' conscious-ness. What defines this consciousness, according to Hegel, is its antagonism to 'the external power of society'—the wish to be free of imposed social circumstances. The English belonged to an earlier historical development, in which Spirit manifests itself as the 'honest soul' whose relation to society is one of 'obedient service' and 'inner reverence'. As Hegel represents the 'disintegrated con-sciousness', it is beyond considerations of sincerity. But the 'honest soul' has sincerity as its essence. If, then, we undertake to explain in Hegelian terms the English trait to which Emerson responded so warmly, we must ascribe it to the archaic intractability of the English social organiza-tion: the English sincerity depends upon the English class structure.

And plainly this was the implicit belief of the English novelists of the nineteenth century. They would all of

[1] For an enlightening polemical discussion of Emerson's attitude to social existence, see ch. I ('The Failure of the Fathers') of Quentin Anderson's *The Imperial Self* (New York, 1971).

them appear to be in agreement that the person who accepts his class situation, whatever it may be, as a given and necessary condition of his life will be sincere beyond question. He will be sincere *and* authentic, sincere *because* authentic. Indeed, the novelists understand class to be a chief condition of personal authenticity; it is their assumption that the individual who accepts what a rubric of the Anglican catechism calls his 'station and its duties' is pretty sure to have a quality of integral selfhood. Whether he be Mr. Knightley or Sam Weller or Plantagenet Palliser, the country gentleman or the cockney servant or the Prime Minister, heir of the Duke of Omnium, a man is what he is by virtue of his class membership. His sentiment of being, his awareness of his discrete and personal existence, derives from his sentiment of class.

And the converse was also true. The novelists gave judicious approval to upward social mobility so far as it could be achieved by energy and talent and without loss of probity. But they mercilessly scrutinized those of their characters who were ambitious to rise in the world, vigilant for signs of such weakening of the fabric of personal authenticity as might follow from the abandonment of an original class position. It was their presumption that such weakening was likely to occur; the names given to its evidences, to the indication of diminished authenticity, were snobbery and vulgarity.

To the general sincerity of the English which Emerson finds so pleasing there is one exception that he remarks, and with considerable asperity—these people, he says, have no religious belief and therefore nothing is 'so odious as the polite bows to God' which they constantly make in their books and newspapers. No student of Victorian life will now confirm Emerson in the simplicity with which he describes the state of religious belief in England. It is true

that the present indifference of the English to religion—
apart from the rites of birth, marriage, and death—was
already in train. By the second half of the nineteenth century the working classes of England were almost wholly
alienated from the established Church and increasingly
disaffected from the Nonconformist sects. It was the rare
intellectual who was in any simple sense a believer. The
commitment of the upper classes was largely a social pro-
priety, and Emerson was doubtless right when he described
it as cant. It is possible to say that the great Dissenting sects
of the middle classes were animated as much by social and
political feelings as by personal faith and doctrinal predilections. Still, when all the adverse portents have been
taken into account, the fact remains that religion as a force
in the life of the nation was by no means yet extinct and
not even torpid, what with Low Church and High
Church, Oxford Movement and the unremitting dissi-
dence of Dissent, public trials over doctrine and private
suffering over crises of belief. Christian faith was taken for
granted as an element of virtue; as late as 1888, Mrs.
Humphry Ward, a niece of Matthew Arnold, could
scandalize the nation with her novel, *Robert Elsmere*, the
history of a gifted and saintly young clergyman who finds
Christian doctrine inacceptable; Gladstone himself felt
called upon to review the book at enormous length.

The history of England was bound up with religion,
which still exercised a decisive influence upon the nation's
politics, its social and ethical style, and its intellectual culture. If there was indeed an attenuation of personal faith
which gave rise to the insincerity that Emerson discerned,
among the intellectual classes it had an opposite effect,
making occasion for the exercise of a conscious and strenuous sincerity. The salient character-type of the Victorian
educated classes was formed, we might say, in response to

the loss of religious faith—the non-believer felt under the necessity of maintaining in his personal life the same degree of seriousness and earnestness that had been appropriate to the state of belief; he must guard against falling into the light-minded libertinism of the French—'You know the French . . . ,' Matthew Arnold said. Perhaps the greatest distress associated with the evanescence of faith, more painful and disintegrating than can now be fully imagined, was the loss of the assumption that the universe is purposive. This assumption, which, as Freud says, 'stands and falls with the religious system', was, for those who held it, not merely a comfortable idea but nothing less than a category of thought; its extirpation was a psychic catastrophe. The Victorian character was under the necessity of withstanding this extreme deprivation, which is to say, of not yielding to the nihilism it implied.

How this end might be achieved is suggested by the anecdote about George Eliot—it has become canonical—which F. W. H. Myers relates. On a rainy May evening Myers walked with his famous guest in the Fellows' Garden of Trinity College, Cambridge, and she spoke of God, Immortality, and Duty. God, she said, was inconceivable. Immortality was unbelievable. But it was beyond question that Duty was 'peremptory and absolute'. 'Never, perhaps,' Myers says, 'have sterner accents affirmed the sovereignty of impersonal and unrecompensing Law. I listened and night fell; her majestic countenance turned towards me like a sybil in the gloom; it was as though she withdrew from my grasp the two scrolls of promise, and left me with the third scroll only, awful with inscrutable fate.' Much as George Eliot had withdrawn from her host, she had not, we may perceive, left him with nothing. A categorical Duty—might it not seem, exactly in its peremptoriness and absoluteness, to have been laid down by the universe itself and thus to validate the personal life that obeyed it? Was a categorical Duty wholly without purpose, without *some* end in view, since it so nearly matched one's own inner imperative, which, in the degree that one responded to it, assured one's coherence and selfhood? And did it not license the thought that man and the universe are less alien to each other than they may seem when the belief in God and Immortality are first surrendered?

We cannot but be touched by Myers's little scene, and perhaps the more because we will not fail to perceive the inauthenticity in which it issues: the very hollowness of the affirmation attests to the need it was intended to satisfy. We of our time do not share that need of the Victorians. We are not under the necessity of discovering in the order of the universe, in the ineluctable duty it silently lays upon us, the validation of such personal coherence and purposiveness as we claim for ourselves. We do not ask those questions which would suggest that the validation is indeed there, needing only to be discovered; to us they seem merely factitious. But we must feel with those who were impelled to ask them.

Still, with what relief we hear the questions being brushed aside not long after they were put with such urgent hope. 'The first duty in life', said one of the great figures of Victoria's reign, 'The first duty in life is to be as artificial as possible.' And Oscar Wilde went on: 'What the second duty is no one has yet discovered.'

ii

With each passing year the figure of Wilde becomes clearer and larger. Neither his posturing nor his martyrdom now obscures his intellectual significance. Its magnitude is suggested by the view expressed by both André Gide and

Thomas Mann that there is a close affinity between Wilde
and Nietzsche.[1] Certainly in one respect the two men are
close to each other: both expressed a principled antagonism
to sincerity, both spoke in praise of what they call the mask.

Wilde, of course, teases the idea of sincerity as one of the
cherished attributes of Philistine respectability. Yet something more than a social polemic is being waged when he
says, for example, that 'all bad poetry springs from genuine
feeling'. He does not mean merely that most genuine feeling
is dull feeling, nor even that genuine feeling needs the
mediation of artifice if it is to be made into good poetry.
He means that the direct conscious confrontation of experience and the direct public expression of it do not necessarily yield the truth and indeed that they are likely to
pervert it. 'Man is least himself', Wilde said, 'when he
talks in his own person. Give him a mask and he will tell
you the truth.' Emerson had not been deterred from his praise
of English sincerity by his having given expression to the
same thought in his Journal for 1840. 'There is no deeper
dissembler', he said, 'than the sincerest man', and in the
following year, 'Many men can write better in a mask than
for themselves.' Nietzsche, whose admiration of Emerson
is always an engaging surprise, says with much the same
intention: 'Every profound spirit needs a mask.'

The mask is justified for Nietzsche by the nature of the
only universe with which he is concerned—the universe
of history and culture. 'It seems', he says, 'that all great

[1] This is remarked by Richard Ellmann in the introduction to his selection
of Wilde's critical writings, *The Artist as Critic* (New York and London,
1970). Gide brings the two names together in a casual and limited way in
the commemoration of Wilde he wrote in 1902, but Mann, after expressing
some anxiety about venturing on the comparison—'Of course there is something almost sacrilegious about the juxtaposition of Nietzsche and Wilde...
—develops it in considerable detail ('Nietzsche's Philosophy in the Light
of Recent History', *Last Essays*, New York and London, 1959).

things first bestride the earth in monstrous and frightening masks in order to inscribe themselves in the hearts of humanity with eternal demands: dogmatic philosophy was such a mask; so also was the Vedanta doctrine in Asia and Platonism in Europe.' Wilde, without ranging so far, says something of similar import in the concluding sentences of his essay, 'The Truth of Masks': '. . . In art there is no such thing as a universal truth. A truth in art is that whose contradictory is also true. And just as it is only in art-criticism, and through it, that we can apprehend the Platonic theory of ideas, so it is only in art-criticism, and through it, that we can realize Hegel's system of contraries. The truths of metaphysics are the truths of masks.'

Irony is one of those words, like love, which are best not talked about if they are to retain any force of meaning—other such words are sincerity and authenticity—but something must be said about it in connection with Wilde and Nietzsche, for the doctrine of masks proposes the intellectual value of the ironic posture. The etymology of the word associates it directly with the idea of the mask, for it derives from the Greek word for a dissembler. It is used in a diversity of meanings,[1] of which the simplest is saying one thing when another is meant, not for the purpose of deceit and not wholly for the purpose of mockery (although this is usually implicit), but, rather, in order to establish a disconnection between the speaker and his interlocutor, or between the speaker and that which is being spoken about, or even between the speaker and himself. Hegel in his *Phenomenology* goes far towards explaining the intellectual value that irony may be supposed to have. Commenting on the extravagant histrionism of Rameau's Nephew, as he assumes an endless succession of roles or, as we may say, masks, Hegel expresses admiration for the

[1] For a succinct explication of them, see Fowler's *Modern English Usage*.

Nephew because through his performance Spirit has been able to 'pour scornful laughter on existence, on the confusion pervading the whole, and on itself as well'. Hegel means, surely, that through that scornful laughter Spirit has gained a measure of freedom—the kind of freedom which we call detachment. If 'existence' is responded to as if it were less than totally in earnest, Spirit is the less bound by it. It can then without sadness accept existence, and without resentment transact such business with it as is necessary. If 'the whole' is seen as 'confused' rather than as orderly and rational, as, in George Eliot's words, peremptory and absolute, the human relation to it need not be fixed and categorical; it can be mercurial and improvisational.

Wilde's aphorism, 'The truths of metaphysics are the truths of masks', can be taken to mean that it is not the philosophical treatise but the work of art which provides the model of the process by which we gain knowledge of existence—it is the work of art which best exemplifies the detachment achieved through irony. Schiller has in mind a similar advantage for the heuristic enterprise when he says in the *Aesthetic Letters* that one of the beneficences of art is that it overcomes 'the earnestness of duty and destiny'. Schiller presents the 'mere play' of the aesthetic experience as the activity of man's true being. 'Man only plays', he says, 'when he is in the fullest sense of the word a human being, and he is only fully a human being when he plays', and presumably the fullness of humanity includes the knowledge of existence. The moral earnestness with which Schiller investigates the possibility of man's liberation from the earnestness of duty and destiny must check any lingering disposition we may have to see Wilde's position as an overture to nihilism. We are further reassured on this score by the affinity between Wilde and Nietzsche, for Nietzsche's hostility to nihilism is settled and explicit.

The human autonomy which is envisioned by Schiller, Wilde, and Nietzsche is, we perceive, in essential accord with the conception of the moral life proposed by Rousseau and Wordsworth when they assigned so high a significance to the sentiment of being. Indeed, the preoccupation with being informs most speculation about the moral life throughout the nineteenth century. The intense meaning which Wordsworth gave to the word 'be' became its common meaning in moral discourse. And it came commonly to be felt that *being*, which is to say the gratifying experience of the self as an entity, was susceptible to influences which either increased or diminished its force. There was a pretty clear consensus, for example, that among the things which increased the experience of self art was pre-eminent. And there was no question at all of what diminished the experience of self—the great enemy of being was *having*. 'The less you eat, drink, buy books, go to the theatre or to balls, or to the public house, and the less you think, love, theorize, sing, paint, fence, etc., the more you will be able to save and the *greater* will become your treasure which neither moth nor dust will corrupt—your *capital*. The less you *are* . . . the more you *have*. . . .' It is accumulation that robs you of being.

No one in Europe in the nineteenth century read the words I have just quoted. It is a passage from Karl Marx's *Economic and Philosophical Manuscripts*, which were written in 1844 but not published until 1932. Since then, however, they have aroused great interest because they disclose a young Marx—he was twenty-six—who may be thought different from, even at variance with, the Marx of the later agitational, polemical, and systematic writings. The mind of the young Marx is more humanistic, in the sense of being less ambitious of scientific rectitude, than that of the author of the canonical works. An index to the humanistic quality of the *Manuscripts* is the emphasis put upon alienation, and not merely the alienation of the working class but that of human beings in general, even of the middle class. Indeed, a member of the middle class might read what Marx says about alienation as having a special and direct bearing on his own bourgeois life. 'The less you *are*, the less you express your life, the more you *have*, the greater is your alienated life—the greater is the saving of your alienated being. Everything which the economist takes from you in the way of life and humanity, he restores to you in the form of *money* and *wealth*. And everything which you are unable to do, your money can do for you; it can eat, drink, go to the ball and the theatre. It can acquire art, learning, historical treasures, political power, and it can travel. It *can* appropriate all these things for you . . . but although it can do all this, it only *desires* to create itself, and to buy itself. . . .'

It will readily be seen that alienation does not mean to Marx what it meant to Hegel. It is not the estrangement of the self from the self, which Hegel sees as a painful but necessary step in development. Rather, it is the transformation of the self into what is not human. Marx's concept of alienation is not wholly contained in what he says about money; but certainly money is central to it and provides the most dramatic way of representing it. In the *Manuscripts*, as later in *Capital*, Marx speaks of money as imbued with a life of its own, a devilish autonomous energy. In him, and in Engels too, there is a strong nostalgic streak which makes them always a little tender of archaic societies in which money is not dominant, and the antiSemitism of both men has its source in the Jewish connection with money and banking. They are likely to be as anxious as any medieval or Renaissance man about the workings of the moneydevil. It is Shakespeare whom Marx quotes—

Goethe also, but to less effect—in support of the idea that money inverts moral values and even perception itself; he cites the speech in which Timon says that money makes 'black, white; foul, fair; / Wrong, right; base, noble; old, young; coward, valiant'.

Money, in short, is the principle of the inauthentic in human existence. 'If I have no money for travel, I have no *need*—no real and self-realizing need—for travel. If I have a *vocation* for study but no money for it, then I have no vocation, i.e. no *effective, genuine* vocation. Conversely, if I really have *no* vocation for study but have money and the urge for it, then I have an *effective* vocation.' And the section of the *Manuscripts* on money ends with these words: 'Let us assume *man* to be *man*, and his relation to the world a human one. Then love can only be exchanged for love, trust for trust, etc. If you wish to enjoy art you must be an artistically cultivated person; if you wish to influence other people you must be a person who really has a stimulating and encouraging effect upon others. Every one of your relations to man and to nature must be a *specific expression* corresponding to the object of your will, of your *real individual* life.'

'Let us assume *man* to be *man*, and his relation to the world a human one.' It is an astounding thing to say: in no other epoch of history had it been felt necessary to make that assumption explicit. Through the nineteenth century runs the thread of anxiety that man may not be man, that his relation to the world may cease to be a human one. Marx's expression of the anxiety was of singular intensity; but one need not have been of his political persuasion to share the apprehension. The perception that being was threatened by having was characteristic of the bourgeois moralists of the age. 'Culture', said Matthew Arnold, 'is not a having but a being and a becoming.' And Oscar

Wilde, in his great essay, 'The Soul of Man under Social-ism', echoed Arnold: 'The true perfection of man lies not in what man has but what man is.' Just as over the portal of the antique world there was written the Delphic maxim, 'Know thyself', just so, Wilde says, 'over the portal of the new world "Be thyself" shall be written'. And Ruskin said, 'There is no wealth but life'.

But it was of course not enough simply to set being over against having and to assert that the one is to be preferred to the other. After all, men may choose to have and yet not choose not to be. And the commitment to having could not be thought the sole cause of the diminution of the sentiment of being which the nineteenth century was aware of—there were in addition causes of an insidious, scarcely discernible kind. The word 'culture' as we now use it was not yet current—the 'culture' that Matthew Arnold opposed to 'anarchy' of course means something else—but the idea of culture in its chief present-day mean-ing was rapidly becoming available: the idea, that is to say, of a unitary complex of interacting assumptions, modes of thought, habits, and styles, which are connected in secret as well as overt ways with the practical arrangements of a society and which, because they are not brought to consciousness, are unopposed in their influence over men's minds. We nowadays take the idea of culture for granted; in the nineteenth century Taine could announce it as a discovery of the age.

How much complexity and even contradiction the idea of culture can encompass is suggested by a curious passage in *English Traits*. In the first of two consecutive paragraphs, Emerson makes one of his laudatory statements about the autonomy and sincerity of the English: 'They require you to be of your own opinion, and they hate the coward who cannot in practical affairs answer yes or no. They dare to

displease, nay, they will let you break all the rules if you
do it natively and with spirit. You must be somebody;
then you may do this or that as you will.' In the next para,
graph, with no transition and with no apparent awareness
of the contradiction, he says: 'Machinery has been applied
to all work and carried to such perfection that little is left
for the men but to mind the engines and feed the furnaces.
But the machines require punctual service, and as they
never tire they prove too much for their tenders. Mines,
forges, mills, breweries, railroads, steam-pump, steam-
plough, drill of regiments, drill of police, rule of court and
shop-rule are operated to give a mechanical regularity to
all the habit and action of men. A terrible machine has
possessed itself of the ground, the air, the men and the
women, and hardly even thought is free.'

Emerson is not talking about an over-driven working
class, nor about actual machine-tending, which would
scarcely have involved the nation as a whole. At a time to
which we of today look back with nostalgia, so innocent
of mechanism does it still seem, he is remarking an influence
which the machine, or the idea of the machine, exerts on
the conduct of life, imposing habits and modes of thought
which make it ever less possible to assume that man is
man, and he utters this observation in the same breath in
which he speaks of the culture's characteristic demand that
one 'be somebody'.

The anxiety about the machine is a commonplace in
nineteenth-century moral and cultural thought: Marx's
'Let us assume *man* to be *man*' means 'Let us assume man
to be not a machine'. The mind is not to be a machine,
not even that part of it which we call reason. The universe
is not to be a machine; the thought that it might be drove
Carlyle to the verge of madness. It was the mechanical
principle, quite as much as the acquisitive principle—the

two are of course intimately connected—which was felt to be the enemy of being, the source of inauthenticity.

The machine, said Ruskin, could make only inauthentic things, dead things; and the dead things communicated their deadness to those who used them. Nor, in his view, is it only actual machinery which produces dead objects, but any mode of making that does not permit the maker to infuse into the artefact the quality of his being. The architecture of ancient Egypt, according to Ruskin, was mechanical because 'servile'—the workman carried out, not his own intention, but that of the master architect. And in the face of the settled opinion of his day Ruskin passed a similar adverse judgement upon the architecture of ancient Greece, not sparing even the sacrosanct Parthenon. Only Gothic architecture was exempt from his blame: it alone among the great styles had the quality of life. On the basis of how the nineteenth century believed the cathedrals to have been built, Ruskin was able to regard them as the embodiment both of the individual and the communal spirit—they were constructed so slowly that it was as if they grew rather than were made, fulfilling not a plan but an entelechy, reaching completion by the inherent laws of their being. Like Goethe in his famous meditation on the tower of Strasbourg, Ruskin cherished the Gothic cathedrals because they were organic. Living things made the elements of their decoration, and their structure depended upon reciprocating energies, which to the responsive eye might manifest themselves as movement.

The belief that the organic is the chief criterion of what is authentic in art and life continues, it need hardly be said, to have great force with us, the more as we become alarmed by the deterioration of the organic environment. The sense of something intervening between man and his own organic endowment is a powerful element in the

modern consciousness, an overt and exigent issue in our
culture. In an increasingly urban and technological society,
the natural processes of human existence have acquired a
moral status in the degree that they are thwarted. It is the
common feeling that some inhuman force has possessed
our ground and our air, our men and women and our
thought, a machine more terrible than any that Emerson
imagined. In many quarters, whatever can be thought
susceptible of analogy to the machine, even a syllogism
or a device of dramaturgy, is felt to be inimical to the
authenticity of experience and being.

Yet in our artistic culture, although the line of partisan⁄
ship with the organic is both long and firm—the names of
D. H. Lawrence, E. M. Forster, Henry Miller, and Samuel
Beckett will suggest something of its not quite simple
direction—the modern aesthetic movement must be under⁄
stood to have derived much of its original energy from a
sudden impatience with the idea of the organic. In his
valuable history of design in what he calls the 'First
Machine Age', Reyner Banham notes the moment when
the world of technology ceased to be regarded with
hostility, at least by a significant number of artists and
intellectuals, and he sums up this new tendency by refer⁄
ence to its antagonism to Ruskin: 'If there is a test that
divides the men from the boys in, say, 1912,' Mr. Banham
says, 'it is their attitude to Ruskin. Men whose views of
the aims of art and the function of design were as diverse
as could be, nevertheless united in their hatred of *ce
déplorable Ruskin*.' Mr. Banham takes the pejorative epithet
from a lecture which Marinetti gave in London to the
Lyceum Club in 1912. The Futurist Manifesto, which
Marinetti wrote and published in 1908, is generally re⁄
garded as the charter for aesthetic modernism as a whole,
even for those movements upon which its principles had

no direct influence. The central doctrine of the Manifesto is the beauty and vitality of the machine; in his London lecture Marinetti denounced Ruskin for the absurdity of his opposition to this truth. 'When, then,' he demanded of his audience, 'will you disencumber yourselves of the lymphatic ideology of your deplorable Ruskin, whom I intend to make utterly ridiculous in your eyes. . . .' And he went on, 'With his sick dream of a primitive pastoral life: with his nostalgia for Homeric cheeses and legendary spinning-wheels; with his hatred of the machine, of steam and electricity, this maniac for antique simplicity resembles a man who in full maturity wants to sleep in his cot again and drink at the breasts of a nurse who has now grown old. . . .'

Marinetti, that is, imputes to the organic as a social and moral ideal exactly the quality of inauthenticity against which the organic principle had itself been directed; not the organic but the mechanical is to be the authenticating principle of modern life. Yet this puts it too simply and perhaps misleadingly. We tend to assume that the principle of the machine necessarily involves a submission to dull regularity and the loss of all gratuitous impulse, of all creative power; we forget that one of the great minds of the modernist movement chose to call his artist-hero by the name of the first engineer: Daedalus designed not only the imprisoning labyrinth but also the wings by which he outsoared his confinement. As Mr. Banham points out, Marinetti may have celebrated the machine in general but it is specifically the automobile that engages the enthusiasm of his Manifesto: in 1908 this is the machine which the individual himself controls and through which he ex-presses his will; it makes him what Freud calls a 'prosthetic God'; it gives him the gift of speed. The fifth proposition of the Futurist Manifesto is that the Movement is to 'hymn

the man at the steering-wheel whose ideal axis passes
through the centre of the earth'.

As the tenor of the Manifesto suggests, the modern
theory of art ascribes peremptoriness and absoluteness not
to the universe but to the creative faculty of the artist.
There are occasions when Ruskin's aesthetic theory almost
seems to depart from its usual course to do the same thing—
the chapter of the second volume of *Modern Painters* called
'Of Imagination Penetrative' speaks of the 'highest
imaginative faculty' as a headlong force which, indifferent
to the outer crust of mere appearance, 'plunges into the
very central fiery heart, nothing else will content its
spirituality, whatever semblances and various outward
shows and phases its subject may possess, go for
nothing. . . .' And the practice of his adored Turner, to
the extent that it exemplifies the imagination penetrative,
seems to contradict Ruskin's characteristic insistence that
the artist's power derives from his submission to the natural
order—Turner's line of development seems to us to be in
the direction of an ever greater autonomy which culminates
in the marvellous oil sketches of his last years: these seem
so little representational, so exempt from the sanction of the
natural order, that they have been compared with the work
of the action painters. Yet the critics who make this comparison have no doubt that even at this stage of his art
Turner was wholly committed to the interpretation of
nature and to the expression of his profound feelings about
its relation to man.[1] Even when he seems wholly autonomous, he is not in fact inventing but discovering. However

[1] I refer to John Rothenstein and Martin Butlin, *Turner* (London, 1964),
pp. 73 and 76. A few of the late sketches were exhibited for the first time in 1906
but they were not shown in any considerable number until 1938. Several
rooms in the Tate Gallery are now devoted to them. It might be observed that
the speed by which Marinetti set store is celebrated in Turner's stunning picture
of 1844, 'Rain, Steam, and Speed—The Great Western Railway'.

imperious in its energies the imagination penetrative may be, it is subdued to this function. And it was not to the purpose of discovery that the leaders of the great modern movement of art directed their powers. They did indeed grant that the natural universe was there and they gave it a degree of notice, but they refused to be submissive and dutiful to it. They poured mocking laughter upon it: they dealt with it in irony and detachment, under no assumption that it was in earnest, that it had promises to keep or any disposition to allow the truth about itself to be discovered, if indeed there was any truth inherent in it. Yet truth, such truth as Schiller, Wilde, and Nietzsche saw in art, might nevertheless follow upon their dealing with the universe in the peculiarly human spirit of play. In that spirit the universe might be taken apart and put together in a new way.

The procedures of the great movement of art of the early century may serve to put us in mind of the violent meanings which are explicit in the Greek ancestry of the word 'authentic'. *Authenteo*: to have full power over; also, to commit a murder. *Authentes*: not only a master and a doer, but also a perpetrator, a murderer, even a self-murderer, a suicide. These ancient and forgotten denotations bear upon the nature and intention of the artistic culture of the period we call Modern. Our habituation to this artistic culture over the decades leads us to speak of it as classic, not only as a way of asserting its greatness but also to express our perception of its qualities of order and repose, even of transcendence. Sometimes we are a little puzzled to under-stand why this art was greeted upon its first appearance with so violent a resistance, forgetting how much violence there was in its creative will, how ruthless an act was required to assert autonomy in a culture schooled in duty and in obedience to peremptory and absolute law, and how

extreme an exercise of personal will was needed to over⁄
come the sentiment of non⁄being.

What does it mean not to be? Herman Melville explicates
the condition in the story which he described as 'A Tale of
Wall Street'. Bartleby lives at the centre of power of the
New World and 'prefers not to' have even so much of
power as will keep him alive, not to permit anything to
evoke his desire or effort; his response to what has become
for him the total inauthenticity of the social world is to
lie down in his isolation and die. *Little Dorrit*, Dickens's
great portrayal of what he regards as the total inauthenticity
of England, has for its hero a man who says of himself, 'I
have no will'. Balzac and Stendhal passionately demon⁄
strated the social inauthenticity which baffles and defeats
the will of their young protagonists. By the time Flaubert
wrote *L'Éducation sentimentale* the defeat could be taken for
granted—the will of Frédéric Moreau was infected by the
culture virtually at his birth; his existence is nothing but the
experience of the duplicity of every human enterprise. Love,
friendship, art, and politics—all are hollow. 'Let us assume
man to be *man*'—but Tolstoy says that no such assumption
can be made of Ivan Ilych until the moment of his dying.

Surely something not less than violent was needed to
startle this dull pain of the social world and make it move
and live, to retrieve the human spirit from its acquiescence
in non⁄being. It needed the perpetration of acts of unpre⁄
cedented power and mastery, such as the acceleration of the
racing car celebrated by Marinetti, whose 'ideal axis passes
through the centre of the earth', a new energy, in immediacy
and swiftness more that of the mobile machine than that of
the gradual processes proposed by the organicist ideal. But
the organic might be permitted if it was sufficiently feral,
like Nijinsky's unprecedented levitations, his sudden leaps
upward and out of sight of the audience, or the murderous

tiger-leap of the actor Di Grasso which Isaac Babel made the symbol of all true art. Or like Kurtz's plunge downward from light into darkness. It was the perpetration of this terrible deed that gave Kurtz the right to affirm the authenticity of life, which he did by articulating its horror. He spoke it with his last breath: 'The horror! The horror!'[1] 'This is the reason', Marlow says, 'why I affirm Kurtz was a remarkable man. He had something to say. He said it. . . . He had summed up—he had judged. "The horror!" He was a remarkable man. . . . I like to think that my summing-up would not have been a word of careless contempt. Better his cry—much better. It was an affirmation, a moral victory paid for by innumerable defeats, by abominable terrors, by abominable satisfactions. But it was a victory! That is why I have remained loyal to Kurtz to the last. . . .'

[1] It is not uncommon for critics of liberal or radical view to interpret Kurtz's last words as a characterization of imperialism, but of course there is no ground for this.

VI · THE AUTHENTIC UNCONSCIOUS

i

ALTHOUGH IN THESE PAGES I HAVE DEALT with authenticity as a criterion of art and as a quality of the personal life which may be either enhanced or diminished by art, I have thus far given scant attention to the specific developments in our contemporary arts by which the preoccupation with authenticity expresses itself. One such development which has taken place in literature will serve as a sufficiently striking example—the drastic reduc⁄tion in the status of narration, of telling stories. It is the exceptional novelist today who would say of himself, as Henry James did, that he 'loved the story as story', by which James meant the story apart from any overt idea⁄tional intention it might have, simply as, like any primitive tale, it brings into play what he called 'the blessed faculty of wonder'. Already in James's day, narration as a means by which the reader was held spellbound, as the old phrase put it, had come under suspicion. And the dubiety grew to the point where Walter Benjamin could say some three decades ago that the art of story⁄telling was moribund. T. S. Eliot's famous earlier statement, that the novel had reached its end with Flaubert and James, would seem to be not literally true; the novel does seem to persist in some sort of life. But we cannot fail to see how uneasy it is with the narrative mode, which once made its vital principle, and how its practitioners seek by one device or another to evade or obscure or palliate the act of *telling*.

Benjamin speaks of the 'orientation towards practical interests' which is 'characteristic of many born story-tellers'; he says that stories are likely to contain, openly or latently, 'something useful', that they have 'counsel to give'. And this giving of counsel, Benjamin says, has come to have 'an old-fashioned ring'. *Old-fashioned*: which is to say in-authentic for the present time—there is something inauthen-tic for our time in being held spellbound, momentarily forgetful of oneself, concerned with the fate of a person who is not oneself but who also, by reason of the spell that is being cast, is oneself, his conduct and his destiny bearing upon the reader's own By what right, we are now inclined to ask, does the narrator exercise authority over that other person, let alone over the reader: by what right does he arrange the confusion between the two and presume to have counsel to give?

Richard Gilman, perhaps with Benjamin's essay in mind, has said of narration that it is 'precisely that element of fiction which coerces and degrades it into a mere alter-native to life, like life, only better of course, a dream (or a serviceable nightmare), a way out, a recompense, a blue-print, a lesson'. A chief part of the inauthenticity of narra-tion would seem to be its assumption that life is susceptible of comprehension and thus of management. It is the nature of narration to explain; it cannot help telling how things are and even why they are that way. How did death come into the world and all that woe? Well, I will tell you— 'In the beginning . . .' But a beginning implies an end, with something in the middle to connect them. The begin-ning is not merely the first of a series of events; it is the event that originates those that follow. And the end is not merely the ultimate event, the cessation of happening; it is a significance or at least the promise, dark or bright, of a significance. The tale is not told by an idiot but by a rational consciousness which perceives in things the processes that are their reason and which derives from this perception a principle of conduct, a way of living among things. Can we, in this day and age, submit to a mode of explanation so primitive, so flagrantly Aristotelean?

To that question a negative answer has been given by a significant part of one important intellectual profession—of recent years many historians have repudiated the ancient allegiance of their craft to the narrative mode. Such is the extent of their disaffection that G. R. Elton can speak of it as 'contemptuous hostility' and feel under the necessity of making the defence of narration a chief intention of his book on the principles and practice of political history. Professor Elton accounts for the settled antagonism to the method of narration by the multiplicity of evidential material which has become available to modern historians. It is a multiplicity so great as to induce the belief that history must inevitably be betrayed into simplicity if it is presented as a story and that 'the only way of writing history consists in taking a bit of the past to pieces before the reader's eyes and putting it together again, in the description of an organism or structure'. Elton acknowledges the intellectual gratification which follows from using the method of structural analysis—'a task properly completed and a piece of proper understanding added . . . to the general store of knowledge'; by comparison, he says, 'the satisfaction of telling a story (however complicated), is likely to be at best aesthetic, at worst meretricious'. Yet he contends that the exclusive commitment to the method of analysis issues in the negation of history itself, for it ignores the 'fact of motion' in which history consists. 'Without a sense of time and change, of life and death, history ceases altogether to be history, whereas a narrative devoid of the full range of past experience is still history, only not altogether adequate or satisfactory history.'

Inevitably we wonder whether it is not something more than considerations of technique that has led the historians to their adverse view of narration, whether beneath the methodological reasons there is not to be discerned an un⁄ formulated cultural judgement. This possibility is affirmed by J. H. Plumb, whose assessment of the low status of narrative history is much more drastic than Elton's: it is his view that the past itself is on the point of being extir⁄ pated from the consciousness of modern man. The extremity of his thesis is announced by the title of the book in which he sets it forth, *The Death of the Past*. 'Industrial society,' Professor Plumb says, 'unlike the commercial, craft and agrarian societies which it replaces, does not need the past. Its intellectual orientation is towards change rather than conservation, towards exploitation and consumption. The new methods, new processes, new forms of living of scientific and industrial society have no sanction in the past and no roots in it. The past becomes, therefore, a matter of curiosity, of nostalgia, of sentimentality.' That is to say, the past, so far as it exists in the modern consciousness at all, is not what until recently it has been—it is not the sanction of authority, it is not the assurance of destiny.[1] Its coming to the verge of death was a sudden event, occurring within present memory, a generation ago—in Britain, Plumb says, the last potency of the past was expressed in the nation's 'concept of its own role in the titanic struggle against Hitler'.

'A narrative past, a past with sharp and positive begin⁄ nings'—it is thus that Plumb characterizes the past that is now vanishing. 'In the beginning God created the heaven

---

[1] Purposes which are served, it is plain, by the newly emerged Black history, which is strongly committed to narration.

and the earth.' 'In the beginning was the Word, and the
Word was with God, and the Word was God.' These are
beginnings as sharp and positive as any can be, and the
great efflorescence of history in the eighteenth and nineteenth centuries—of narrative history, as now we are required to say—may be thought to have had as one of its
unavowed aims to supply their loss. When God died, as
by common consent he did, however slowly the explicit
news of the demise reached us, history undertook to provide
the beginnings which men once thought necessary to the
authenticity of the world and themselves. Nietzsche says that
the realization of the death of God had the effect of making
all things, and man himself, seem 'weightless': the great
narrative historians in some considerable degree maintained
the weightiness of things by thickening the past, making it
exigent, imperative, a sanction of authority, an assurance of
destiny. The tale they told interpreted the sound and fury of
events, made them signify *something*, a direction taken, an
end in view. 'In the beginning was the Witenagemot.' 'In the
beginning was the genius of the Celtic race.' From which
follow the purpose, the glories, the essential rightness, the
indubitable actuality, the firm sentiment of being of the
English people, of the French people. Narrative history, by
its representation of necessity and vicissitude, served to keep
man sufficiently weighty, made it still possible for feet to
know that the solid earth was under them, that there was
a required and right course for them to follow. 'To write
the History of England as a kind of Bible'—this was an
enterprise that Carlyle urged in a time of crisis and anxiety.
'For England too (equally with any Judah whatsoever) has
a History that is Divine; an Eternal Providence presiding
over every step of it . . . ; guiding England forward to *its*
goal and work, which too has been considerable in the
world!'

But now the narrative past, like the divine Beginner for whom it was for a time the surrogate, has lost its authenticating power. Far from being an authenticating agent, indeed, it has become the very type of inauthenticity. *Here* and *now* may be unpleasant, but at least they are authentic in being really here and now, and not susceptible to explanation by some shadowy *there* and *then*. The disfavour into which narrative history has fallen with historians is reflected in its virtual extirpation from the curriculum of our schools and its demotion in the curriculum of our colleges.[1] It has changed the nature of political thought, the radical no less than the conservative: Marxist theory, so far as it is popular, no longer proceeds under the aegis of the 'logic of history', as so proudly it did forty years ago. It bears upon the extreme attenuation of the authority of literary culture, upon the growing indifference to its traditional pedagogy; the hero, the exemplary figure, does not exist without a sharp and positive beginning; the hero is his history from his significant birth to his significant death. And perhaps the low status of narration can be thought to have a connection with revisions of the child's relation to the family— traditionally the family has been a narrative institution: it was the past and it had a tale to tell of how things began, including the child himself; and it had counsel to give.

ii

I have not put forward the matter of our culture's adverse opinion of narration in order to deal with it as in itself it deserves to be dealt with, but only to exemplify the kind of cultural phenomena which might properly come

---

[1] I refer only to American schools and colleges. What the status of history is in the educational systems of other nations I do not with certainty know, although I venture to suppose that it is lower than it formerly was.

within our purview. But now that it is before us, it may appropriately be made to serve a further purpose, that of introducing a large and difficult subject—the ideal of authenticity as it relates to the modern theory of the mind, and in particular to that concept which is definitive of modern psychological theory, the unconscious. The concept of the unconscious was brought to its present complex development by psychoanalysis. As I need scarcely say, psychoanalysis is a science which is based upon narration, upon telling. Its principle of explanation consists in getting the story told—somehow, anyhow—in order to discover how it begins. It presumes that the tale that is told will yield counsel.

Psychoanalysis entered fully upon the cultural scene not many years before Eliot made his statement about the novel having come to its end. Some critics have speculated that psychoanalysis itself played a part in the devolution of the novel, that it offered a narrative explanation of conduct which, by comparison with that of prose fiction, seemed more complete and authoritative. But if psychoanalysis can be thought to have been in competition with the novel and to have won some sort of ascendancy over it, this was not of long duration. Earlier I remarked on the fact that at present there is a withdrawal of credence from Freudian theory. This development cannot be ascribed to any single cause, but the contemporary disenchantment with narration as a way of explaining things surely has some bearing upon it.

Still, if a withdrawal of credence from psychoanalysis is indeed to be observed as a tendency of our culture, it is one which has by no means completed itself. Among the elements of Freudian theory there is at least one that stands in no danger of being abandoned, for it is integral to our cultural disposition. This is the doctrine that in the human mind there are two systems, one manifest, the other latent or covert. It is not an idea with which we are always at ease—the personal evidences of an unconscious mental system are likely to be received by each of us with an ever fresh surprise and discomfiture which qualify their credibility. Yet despite occasional vicissitudes, the idea of an unconscious mental system is firmly established in our culture.

That a portion of the activity of the mind is not immediately available to consciousness is of course not in itself a new idea. It did not originate with psychoanalysis. Freud himself said that it was the poets who discovered the unconscious, and beyond the poets' instinctive recognition of it there has been a considerable body of formulated belief in its existence and some fairly specific predications about its nature. Scholars have described the numerous pre-Freudian theories of the unconscious and a recent work by Henri F. Ellenberger, *The Discovery of the Unconscious*, does so in an especially thorough way.

In speaking of the sources of Freud's thought, Professor Ellenberger adduces an intellectual tendency which, he says, requires emphasis because it has hitherto been overlooked. This is the disposition of mind, salient in Europe for some centuries, which Ellenberger calls the 'unmasking trend' and describes as 'the systematic search for deception and self-deception and the uncovering of underlying truth'. He assigns its beginnings to the French moralists of the seventeenth century and notes its continuance in Schopenhauer, Marx, Ibsen, and Nietzsche. I have spoken of the important part that the idea of 'unmasking' played in the ethos of the French Revolution. The 'unmasking trend' continues with unabated energy in our own time, and if we try to say why the idea that there is a mental system which lies hidden under the manifest system has won so wide an acceptance among us, doubtless one reason is that it accords with the firmly entrenched belief that beneath the appearance of every human phenomenon there lies concealed a discrepant actuality and that intellectual, practical, and (not least) moral advantage is to be gained by forcibly bringing it to light.

It would be an incomplete but not an inaccurate description of the theory of psychoanalysis to say that it conceives of the conscious system of the mind as a mask for the energies and intentions of the unconscious system. Freud himself puts it that the ego, which is the seat of consciousness, is 'a kind of façade for the id', which is unconscious. This suggests a complicity between the ego and the id, which does in fact exist. It does not, however, suggest the antagonism that also exists between the two entities. The energies and intentions of the id are instinctual and libidinal and its sole aim is the achievement of pleasure. The primary concern of the ego is with the survival of the human organism, and to this end the ego undertakes to control the heedless energies and intentions of the id, going so far as to thrust them out of sight, which is to say, out of consciousness. By thus repressing the impulses of the id, the ego makes possible the existence of society, which is necessary for human survival.

But the tale, as we know all too well, does not end here. The instinctual drives of the id, although controlled and in large part repressed, do not acquiesce in the programme of the ego. In the darkness of the unconscious to which they are relegated, these drives maintain a complex subversive relation with the conscious system and succeed to some extent in expressing themselves through it, not directly but by means of a devious symbolism. This symbolic expression of the repressed instinctual drives typically involves some degree of pain and malfunction and is called neurosis. The pathology is universal among mankind. As Freud puts it, 'We are all ill'—neurosis is of the very nature of the mind. Its intensity varies from individual to individual; in some the pain or malfunction caused by the symbolizing process is so considerable as to require clinical treatment. But the psychic dynamics of such persons are not different from those of the generality of mankind. We are all neurotic.

The clinical procedure of psychoanalysis is well known. The therapeutic method is based on the belief that when once the conscious part of the mind learns to interpret the difficult symbolism of the repressed drives of the uncon⁄scious and by this means brings to light what it feared and thrust out of sight, the ego will be able to confront the drives of the id in all their literalness and thus be relieved of the pain that their symbolic expression causes. The patient, the analysand, by various means—by retrieving his childhood experience, by reporting his dreams and inter⁄preting them with the analyst's help, by articulating his fantasies and his fugitive thoughts, of which some will be trivial and silly, others shameful—will learn to identify the subversive devices of the banished impulses and come to terms with them as appropriate elements of his nature, thus depriving them of their power over him.

The therapeutic process of psychoanalysis would seem to constitute a very considerable effort of self⁄knowledge, a strenuous attempt to identify and overcome in the mental life of the individual an inauthenticity which is not the less to be deplored because it is enforced and universal. And this is so not only by reason of the nature of what has been concealed and is now to be discovered, because, that is, the idea of authenticity readily attaches itself to instinct, especially libidinal instinct, but also because a profound inauthenticity of the mental life is implied by the nature of neurosis, by its being a disguised substitute for something else. Psychoanalysis speaks of the pain or malfunction of neurosis as a 'substitutive gratification'—what could be more inauthentic than an impulse towards pleasure which gains admission into consciousness by masquerading as its opposite? The neurosis is a Tartuffian deceit practised by one part of the mind upon another. It is to be dealt with by a minute investigation of its machinations which will lead to tearing the mask from its face.

This enterprise does not in itself constitute the whole of the psychoanalytical therapy or suggest the full extent of the developed theory of the neurosis. Yet it expresses what might be called the initiating principle of Freud's system and as such it is singled out by Jean-Paul Sartre to bear the brunt of the adverse judgement he passes upon psychoanalysis, which holds that the psychoanalytical enterprise of track-ing down and exposing the inauthenticity of the mental life is itself ineluctably inauthentic.

Sartre delivers this opinion in the well-known second chapter of *Being and Nothingness*, his monumental and com-pulsive research into the conditions of personal authenticity. The chapter is entitled 'Bad Faith', a term which the trans-lator of the work in her 'Key to Special Terminology' defines in part as 'a lie to oneself within the unity of a single consciousness'. The psychoanalytical transaction with the clandestine instinctual drives is said by Sartre to be open to the imputation of this falsehood in two respects. One bears upon the moral consequences of the mental dualism which psychoanalysis assumes, the other upon what may be described as the intentional naiveté with which psychoanalysis interprets the prevarications of the psychic mechanism it postulates.

The dualism to which Sartre refers is that of the uncon-scious id, which is wholly comprised of the instinctual drives, and the conscious ego. 'By the distinction between the "id" and the "ego",' Sartre says, 'Freud has cut the psychic whole into two.' The bad faith of psychoanalysis follows from this dichotomy. It consists of one part of the psychic whole regarding the other part as an object and thereby disclaiming responsibility for it. This disclaimer is implicit in the circumstance that the activities of the id can be known to the ego only by hypothesis, as more or less probable; they cannot be known with the force of an intuition, of a felt experience, as an actual part of the individual's moral being. As Sartre puts it, 'I *am* the ego but I *am not* the id', which is to say, 'I am my own psychic phenomena in so far as I establish them in their conscious reality.' The person in psychoanalytic treatment is inducted into a view of the psyche according to which he, the ego-he, the subject, is to take cognizance of part of his mental life not in its 'conscious reality', not as an intuition, but as an object. The psychic facts which are made manifest to him, although they are represented as being of decisive importance in their effect upon him, he apprehends as external phenomena, having their existence apart from the consciousness which constitutes his being. 'I am not these psychic facts', Sartre says, 'in so far as I receive them passively . . .', that is, in so far as he receives them as objects. And not only are the psychic facts of the id received passively by the ego, they are received with but limited credence—'I am not these psychic facts, in so far as I . . . am obliged to resort to hypotheses about their origin and true meaning, just as the scholar makes conjectures about the nature and essence of an external phenomenon.' The criterion of the truth of these hypotheses is 'the number of conscious psychic facts which it explains', but its explanation can never have the certainty of intuitions. Psychoanalysis, in sum, so far from advancing the cause of personal authenticity, actually subverts it in a radical way through the dichotomy it institutes in the mental life, one of whose elements is consigned to a mere objective existence, hypothetical into the bargain, for which the subject is not answerable.

Presumably it would not weigh with Sartre that psycho⁄analysis in its clinical practice seeks to overcome the dual⁄ism it is said to postulate, making it a desideratum that the psychic facts disclosed to the analysand shall have for him the force of an intuition, of a felt experience, and as such be made part of his subjectivity. Inevitably the extent of the subjectivization falls short of completeness and some part of the psychic facts remains in an unregenerate state of existence as an object.

The second line of argument which Sartre takes in bringing into question the authenticity of psychoanalysis bears upon the nature of the 'censor', which stands between the consciousness of the ego and the subversive libidinal energies of the id and prevents the latter from making themselves directly manifest.[1] This agent of repression is represented by psychoanalysis as belonging to the uncon⁄scious part of the mental life, and it is Sartre's point that this definition of it is false, because in order to carry out its function, the censor must engage in purposive acts of per⁄ception and discrimination which are of the very nature of consciousness. '. . . It is not enough that it discern the condemned drives; it must also apprehend them as *to be repressed*, which implies in it at the very least an awareness of its activity. In a word, how could the censor discern

---

[1] The editors of the Standard Edition of *The Complete Psychological Works of Sigmund Freud* (24 vols., London, 1951–69) are at pains to point out (vol. xvi, p. 429 n. and vol. xxii, p. 15 n.) that only on 'very rare occasions' does Freud use the word *Zensor*, which means 'censor'; commonly—'almost invariably'—he uses the word *Zensur*, which means 'censorship'. The agent of censorship is fully identified in what is said below of the development of Freud's theory of the ego.

the impulses needing to be repressed without consciousness of them? How can we conceive of a knowledge which
is ignorant of itself? To know is to know that one knows,
said Alain. Let us rather say that all knowing is a consciousness of knowing.' The conclusion is that the censor
must have a consciousness of 'being conscious of the drive
to be repressed, but precisely in order not to be conscious of
it'. For psychoanalysis to base its explanations upon an agent
of the mental life to which such double-dealing can be
ascribed is surely bad faith at its worst.[1]

It is to be observed that in *Being and Nothingness* Sartre
deals with the theory of psychoanalysis in a relatively early
stage in its development. Writing in 1943, he takes no
account of the changes that had been going on in Freud's
thought for almost a quarter-century. In 1919 Freud began
a radical revision of his theory of the unconscious, especially
of the ego. The new formulations make anachronistic
Sartre's description of the way Freud cuts the psychic whole
into two, for it can no longer be said that the dichotomy
he institutes is that of the conscious ego and the unconscious id. On the basis of the older theory Sartre had been
justified in understanding the ego to be synonymous with
the conscious self, but in Freud's drastic modification of his
former view the ego is no longer represented as being coextensive with consciousness: some part of the ego is now
said to be as far out of sight in the darkness of the unconscious as the id itself. 'There is something in the ego',
Freud says, 'which is also unconscious, which behaves
exactly like the repressed—that is, which produces powerful effects without being itself conscious and which requires
special work before it is made conscious.'

[1] Sartre's argument, which I have not summarized in its full detail, is directed
to the psychoanalytic explanation of the analysand's 'resistance' to the therapeutic process.

What is more, the ego is no longer viewed as 'something autonomous and unitary' and in this character as wholly antagonistic to the id. Rather, Freud says, the ego in its unconscious part is 'continued without sharp limitation' into the id. 'The ego itself is cathected with libido', and so intimate is the involvement of the two psychic entities, once thought to be nothing but hostile to each other, that Freud can say of the ego that it 'is the libido's home and remains to some extent its headquarters'.

There is yet another modification of the earlier account of the ego. To Freud's surprise—he speaks of the phenomenon as a 'strange' one—the activities which go on in the unconscious part of the ego are the same as some of the activities which the conscious part of the ego characteristically engages in. These are activities which are regarded as, to use Freud's phrase, 'extremely high ones', such as moral judgement and self-criticism.

The momentousness of Freud's revision of his theory of the ego will be immediately apparent. Where once the ego, the segment of the mind which, so to speak, does the living and transacts business with the world, was thought of as wholly conscious and bedevilled in its practical purposive existence by the blind instinctual drives which seek to subvert it, now the ego is understood to be in part unavailable to consciousness, no less devious than the id and profoundly implicated with the id's libidinal energies, while at the same time its 'extremely high' activities of moral judgement and self-criticism direct themselves not only upon the id but also upon the conscious part of itself.

There would seem to be no element of the new theory, supposing Sartre to have been aware of it, which is calculated to qualify his position on the inherent inauthenticity of psychoanalysis. To be sure, we have seen that it can no longer be charged against Freud that he cuts the psychic whole into two in the particular way that Sartre complains of. But if the dualism of subject–ego and object–id has been done away with, we now have the larger and more portentous dualism of conscious ego as subject and unconscious ego as object, with all the import of inau⁄thenticity it has for the phenomenological and existential position, of which Sartre's chapter may stand as the paradigm. As for Freud's having identified the agent of censorship as the unconscious part of the ego, to which he attributes the activities of moral judgement and self⁄criticism, it would seem to confirm Sartre's contention that the unconscious is not properly to be so designated, for by definition these 'extremely high' activities are based upon knowing, which, equally by definition, is consciousness of knowing.

The imputed contradiction cannot be thought a source of distress to the psychoanalytic theory. It may be said, indeed, that the tendency of the later development of Freud's thought is exactly to assign to the unconscious, specifically to the ego, those traits of perception, of knowing, which are implied by intention. If this leads to the necessity of characterizing as conscious what psychoanalysis terms 'the unconscious', the contradiction is one of terminology rather than of conception. The good faith of psychoanalysis is not impugned if the situation it postulates is described as being that of two consciousnesses, one of which is not accessible to the other by intuition.

The increased degree of systematic intentionality which psychoanalysis had discovered in what it designates as the unconscious did not make any the easier the task of bring⁄ing it into the comprehension of what it calls the conscious. On the contrary: the extreme complication of the topo⁄graphy and dynamics of the ego and the 'special work' it called for gave pause to the earlier therapeutic optimism of psychoanalysis, at least in point of the length of time required for successful treatment, leading Freud to write his paper with the disquieting title, 'Analysis Terminable and Interminable'. The increased refractoriness of the unconscious is to be laid at the door of a newly discerned principle of inauthenticity, the extent of whose duplicity is suggested by its success in appropriating the reason and authority of society for its own self-serving purposes. The virtually resistless power of this principle of inauthenticity is the informing idea of Freud's mature social theory.

From the first, it need scarcely be said, a conception of society had been central to Freud's psychology. The ego was a social entity; society was the field of its experience and from society the ego took much of its direction and received many of its gratifications. In relation to the id, which was defined by its a-social impulses, the ego was the surrogate of society. One might say that society was all too rigorous in its demands and that at its hands the ego as well as the id of any of its individual members suffered excessive frustration. Still, the social life had come into being at the behest of the ego and to serve its purpose of survival. The price which society exacted for advancing the aims of the ego could be scrutinized and possibly adjusted. Psychoanalysis certainly did not license the idea that communal life and the civilization that arose from it could be changed in any essential way, to the end of freeing the individual from frustration, yet it did seem to suggest that the relation between the individual and the community was, roughly speaking, a contractual one, which the individual might regard pragmatically. It was a relation that seemed to admit of at least some degree of accommodation on both sides.

But this view of the cause of individual frustration was profoundly modified by the development of Freud's new conception of the ego. In 1930 Freud published his most fully articulated statement of what his theory of the mind implies for man's social destiny. *Civilization and Its Discontents* is a work of extraordinary power. For social thought in our time its significance is unique. It may be thought to stand like a lion in the path of all hopes of achieving happiness through the radical revision of social life.

Despite Freud's gift of lucid expression, *Civilization and Its Discontents* is a difficult book, in some part because it undertakes to lead us beyond an idea with which we are familiar and comfortable, that society is the direct and 'sufficient' cause of man's frustration. Its central thesis is that society is no more than the 'necessary' cause of frustration. As Freud now describes the dynamics of the unconscious, the direct agent of man's unhappiness is an element of the unconscious itself. The requirements of civilization do indeed set in train an exigent disciplinary process whose locus is the ego, but this process, Freud says in effect, is escalated by the unconscious ego far beyond the rational demands of the societal situation. The informing doctrine of *Civilization and Its Discontents* is that the human mind, in the course of instituting civilization, has so contrived its own nature that it directs against itself an unremitting and largely gratuitous harshness.

The specific agent of this extravagant severity is an element of the unconscious which has not been named in what I have so far said about psychoanalysis, although its activities have been referred to—they are those 'extremely high ones' of moral judgement and self-criticism. The element of the unconscious that carries on these activities Freud calls the superego. He tells us that the superego was originally part of the ego but seceded from it to establish an autonomous existence and a position of dominance over the ego's activities. It derives its authority from society, whose psychic surrogate it in some sense is. In some sense only, however, because in point of repressiveness the super-ego is far more severe than society, whose purposes are largely practical and therefore controlled by reason. We mistake the nature of the superego when we make it exactly synonymous, as we commonly do, with conscience. Only up to a point are the two coextensive. The operations of conscience are determined by its practical social intentions, but the superego is under no such limitation and in consequence its activity is anything but rational.[1] The process it has instituted against the ego is largely gratuitous, beyond the needs of reason and beyond the reach of reason. The particular kind of pain it inflicts is that which Freud calls guilt.

We must be clear that in Freud's use of it this notorious word does not have its ordinary meaning. Freud does not use it to denote the consciousness of wrong-doing, which he calls remorse.[2] The nature of guilt as Freud conceives it is precisely that it does not originate in actual wrong-doing and that it is not conscious. It takes its rise from an un-fulfilled and repressed wish to do wrong, specifically the wrong of directing aggression against a sacrosanct person, originally the father, and it is experienced not as a discrete and explicit emotion but as the negation of emotion, as anxiety and depression, as the diminution of the individual's powers and the perversion of the intentions of his conscious ego, as the denial of the possibility of gratification and

[1] For the complex distinctions that Freud makes between conscience and the superego, see, for example, *Civilization and Its Discontents*, Standard Edition, vol. xxi (London, 1963), p. 136.

[2] See ibid., p. 131. 'When one has a sense of guilt after having committed a misdeed, and because of it, the feeling should more properly be called *remorse*. It relates only to a deed that has been done. . . .' See also pp. 132, 134 (on the 'normality' of remorse), 136–7.

delight, even of desire. Guilt is Blake's worm at the root of the rosetree.

At this point I think it should be remarked that the description of the superego given in *Civilization and Its Discontents* is—by conscious intention, of course—a highly prejudicial one, putting all possible emphasis upon the gratuitousness of its behaviour, upon its lack of measure and reason, its needless harshness. As against this pejorative view, we should recall that Freud understood the institution of the superego to be a decisive 'advance' in the development of the mind. 'It is in keeping with the course of human development that external coercion gradually becomes internalized,' he says in *The Future of an Illusion*; 'for a special mental agency, man's superego, takes it over.... Every child presents this process of transformation to us; only by that means does it become a moral and social being. Such a strengthening of the superego is a most precious cultural asset in the psychological field. Those in whom it has taken place are turned from being opponents of civilization into being its vehicles. The greater their number is in a cultural unit the more secure is its culture and the more it can dispense with external measures of coercion.'

Yet when we have given all possible recognition to the essential and beneficent part that the superego plays in the creation and maintenance of civilized society, we cannot ignore its deplorable irrationality and cruelty. These traits manifest themselves in an ultimate form in the terrible paradox that although the superego demands renunciation on the part of the ego, every renunciation which the ego makes at its behest, so far from appeasing it, actually increases its severity. The aggression which the ego surrenders is appropriated by the superego to intensify its own aggression against the ego, an aggression which has no motive save that of its own aggrandizement. The more the ego submits to the superego, the more the superego de-mands of it in the way of submission.

It is not practicable to recapitulate here Freud's explana-tion of how the superego became what it now is—the argument is difficult in the extreme, involving as it does the contradictions and conversions of the immemorial dia-lectic between the fostering and unifying instinct which Freud calls Eros and the hypothesized death-instinct from which aggression derives.[1] And for our purpose, the whole of the dark history, fascinating though it be, is not essential. It will be enough if we understand that although it was to serve the needs of civilization that the superego was installed in its disciplinary office, its actual behaviour was not dictated by those needs; the movement of the superego from rational pragmatic authority to gratuitous cruel tyranny was wholly autonomous.

This being so, must we not say that Freud's theory of the mind and of society has at its core a flagrant inauthenticity which it deplores but accepts as essential in the mental structure? Man's existence in civilization is represented as being decisively conditioned by a psychic entity which, under the mask of a concern with social peace and union, carries on a ceaseless aggression to no purpose save that of the enhancement of its own power, inflicts punishment for no act committed but only for a thought denied, and, so far from being appeased by acquiescence in its demands, actually increases its severity in the degree that it is obeyed. Nor does the insatiable tyrant confine its operations to the internal life of individuals; its rage for peaceableness

[1] It is perhaps worth observing that although subsequent writers, taking licence from Freud's use of Eros. often refer to the death-instinct as Thanatos, Freud himself does not use the Greek word, perhaps because he wished the speculative and much-resisted concept to carry the unmediated force of common speech.

quickens and rationalizes man's rage against man. The hegemony of this ferocious idol of the psychic cave may indeed not have been required or intended by civilization, but surely in tolerating the great fraud civilization is profoundly implicated in its grotesque inauthenticity.

It is natural to suppose that if this anomalous condition of human existence can be discovered and described by the rational intellect, it might, by this same agency, be dealt with to the end of controlling its activity and thus bringing about a substantial increase of human happiness. Inevitably we entertain the speculation that, since the aggressivity of the superego has some part of its tortuous etiology in its response to the aggressive impulses of the ego, a revision of societal arrangements which would have the effect of lessening ego-aggression might induce the superego to abate its characteristic fierceness. Freud himself, in the concluding pages of *Civilization and Its Discontents*, raises the question of how far this project is susceptible of being realized. The reply he makes is tentative and gentle in its manner, as how could it not be, denying as it does an aspiration to which all of conscious human desire must tend? He will not dismiss out of hand the possibility of devising societal forms which might have a beneficent effect upon the psychic dynamics he has described. But his scepticism, though muted in courtesy to our hope, is profound—is, we cannot but know, entire. He consents to say that it is 'quite certain that a real change in the relation of human beings to possessions' would make society's ethical ideals more easily attainable. He cannot go on to say that this will bring about a melioration of the dynamics of the unconscious life. He understands the limitless exigence of the superego to be rooted in the timeless past, in the natural history of an organism in which the ceaseless effort to survive is matched in strength by the will to find peace in extinction.

Against the psychic dynamics produced by this ambivalence, this interfusion of the primal Yes and the no less
primal No, and reinforced by later ambivalences such as
the simultaneous love and hate of the father and the desire
both for isolate autonomy and for union with others, it is
unlikely that any revision of societal forms can prevail.
Ultimately it is a given of biology, definitive of man's
nature, and its consequences are not to be reversed.

Why did Freud bring his intellectual life to its climax—
for such we must take *Civilization and Its Discontents* to be
—with this dark doctrine? What was his motive in pressing upon us the ineluctability of the pain and frustration
of human existence?

The question I put is the one that Nietzsche says should
guide our dealings with any systematic thinker. He urges
us to look below the structure of rational formulation to
discover the *will* that is hidden beneath, and expressed
through, its elaborations. What is that will up to? What
does it want—really want, that is, apart from the 'truth'
that it says it wants?

There is no malice in the question Nietzsche prescribes.
It has for its purpose not 'reduction' but comprehension,
such grasp upon a man's thought as may come through
the perception of its unarticulated and even unconscious
intention. It is a mode of critical investigation whose pro-
priety and efficiency Freud himself of course confirms.

To that question I would propose this answer: that
Freud, in insisting upon the essential immitigability of
the human condition as determined by the nature of the
mind, had the intention of sustaining the authenticity of
human existence that formerly had been ratified by God.
It was his purpose to keep all things from becoming
'weightless'.

For Freud, as we know, religion was an illusion with no

future whatever. This certitude was central to his world-view and he was remorseless in his efforts to enforce it. Yet from religion as it vanished Freud was intent upon rescuing one element, the imperative actuality which religion attributed to life. Different individual temperaments, committed to incompatible cultural predilections, will respond to *Civilization and Its Discontents* in diverse ways, but all will take into account, positively or negatively, its powerful representation of the momentous claim which life makes upon us, by very reason, it seems, of its hardness, intractability, and irrationality. The fabric of contradictions that Freud conceives human existence to be is recalcitrant to preference, to will, to reason; it is not to be lightly manipulated. His imagination of the human condition preserves something—much—of the stratum of hardness that runs through the Jewish and Christian traditions as they respond to the hardness of human destiny. Like the Book of Job it propounds and accepts the mystery and the naturalness —the natural mystery, the mysterious naturalness—of suffering. At the same time it has at its heart an explanation of suffering through a doctrine of something like original sin: not for nothing had Freud in his youth chosen John Milton as a favourite poet, and although of course the idea of redemption can mean nothing to him, he yet acquiesces, and with something of Milton's appalled elation, in the ordeal of man's life in history.

Nothing could be further from my intention than to suggest that Freud's attitude to human experience is religious. I have it in mind only to point to the analogy which may be drawn between Freud's response to life and an attitude which, although it is neither exclusive to nor definitive of religion, is yet, as it were, contained in religion and sustained by it. This is what we might call the tragic element of Judaism and Christianity, having reference to the actual literary genre of tragedy and its inexplicable power to activate, by the representation of suffering, a faith quite unrelated to hope, a piety that takes virtually the form of pride—however harsh and seemingly gratuitous a fate may be, the authenticity of its implicit significance is not to be denied, confirmed as it is by the recognition of *some* imperative which has both brought it into being and prescribed its acceptance, and in doing so affirmed the authenticity of him to whom the fate is assigned. It is this authenticating imperative, irrational and beyond the reach of reason, that Freud wishes to preserve. He locates it in the dialectic of Eros and death, which is the beginning of man's nature. Its force in his own life, in the shaping of its character and style, was decisive. In the last days of his long painful illness Freud forbade his physician to administer any anodyne stronger than aspirin, and when he discovered that his injunction had been violated out of compassion, he flashed out in anger, '*Mit welchem Recht?*': *by what right* had the good Dr. Schur interfered with his patient's precious sentiment of being as that was defined by his chosen relation to his fate, with—as a phrase in *Beyond the Pleasure Principle* has it—the organism's 'wish to die in its own way'?[1] That bitter rebuke had its origin in assumptions that are now archaic. The perception of their inevitable anachronism, of their ever-diminishing vitality, was the ground of Nietzsche's revulsion from the developing modern culture. Nietzsche dreaded the 'weightlessness of all things', the inauthenticity of experience, which he foresaw would be the consequence of the death of God. Hence his celebration of what he called the 'energizing pessimism' of the Greeks in their great day, hence his passionate recommendation of *amor fati*, which might be translated by a phrase of Marx's, 'the appropriation of

[1] See the note on p. 183.

human reality' which includes, Marx said, human suffering, 'for suffering humanly considered is an enjoy-ment of the self for man'.

It need scarcely be said that *Civilization and Its Dis-contents* receives scant welcome from the dominant intel-lectual culture of the present time. Its view that life in civilization is largely intractable to reasonable will is pro-foundly alien to the prevailing ideology. Its informing ethos cannot fail to offend the established moral sensibility. The nature of the affront it offers is suggested by its very title. Freud thought first of calling the book *Das Unglück in der Kultur*, 'Unhappiness in Civilization'; this he changed to the present title, *Das Unbehagen in der Kultur*, and suggested that this be translated as 'Man's Discomfort in Culture'; he assented to the phrase by which the book is now known in English. 'Unhappiness' which is a 'discomfort' or a 'discontent'—the understatement proposes a firm accept-ance of life, of death, and of the developed mode of existence which is yielded by the unremitting dialectic between them, but at the same time a cold eye cast upon all three: an irony of simultaneous commitment and detachment such as is required of Aristotle's large-souled man. So patrician an ethical posture cannot fail to outrage the egalitarian hedonism which is the educated middle class's charac-teristic mode of moral judgement.

A clear index of the distance at which the book, and Freudian theory in general, now stand from contemporary sentiment is the attention and admiration which of recent years have been given to the writings of the British psychiatrist, R. D. Laing. Of the complex psychic dynamics which Freud explicated Dr. Laing takes no account whatever. His theory of mental pathology rules out the possibility of pain being inherent in the processes of the mind, and, indeed, gives but limited recognition to any autonomous mental activity. Laing solves the uniquely difficult problem of schizophrenia by assigning to this extreme mental disorder an etiology of ultimate simplicity —schizophrenia, in his view, is the consequence of an external circumstance, an influence exerted upon the psyche, specifically upon the sense of selfhood, of a person who is more disposed than others to yield to it; the schizo-phrenic person characteristically has what Laing calls an 'ontological insecurity', a debility of his sentiment of being. The malignant influence which he fails to withstand com-monly masks itself in benevolence, yet its true nature is easily detected, for it is always the same thing, a pressure exerted by society through the agency of the family. It is the family which is directly responsible for the ontological break, the 'divided self' of schizophrenia; Laing is cate-gorical in saying that every case of schizophrenia is to be understood as 'a special strategy that the patient invents in order to live an unlivable situation', which is always a family situation, specifically the demand of parents that one have a self which is not one's true self, that one be what one is not. We may put it that Laing construes schizo-phrenia as the patient's response to the parental imposition of inauthenticity.

Laing does not say through what conditions there de-velops, or might develop, the personal being which is really one's own, what are the means by which authentic-ity is maintained. Although his theory of mental disorder inculpates society in an ultimate degree, he proposes no revision of present societal arrangements by which mental pathology, or the mental impoverishment which he attri-butes to the state of 'normality' in our culture, might be prevented. The only principle for societal action which may be thought to emerge from Laing's impassioned and sometimes brilliant and moving diagnosis of the given state of affairs is wholly and blandly negative—since the self of the infant can maintain its pristine authenticity only if the process of its maturation is self-determined, it follows that we must not give our assent to any form of rearing, education, or socialization in which prescriptive influence has a part.

What Laing tells us about the mind in relation to society is of course not new in any essential way. It is a view to which, in one degree of intensity or another, our culture has long been habituated. The inculpation of society has become with us virtually a category of thought. We understand *a priori* that the prescriptions of society pervert human existence and destroy its authenticity. The enthusiasm for Laing is a response not to the originality of his conception but to its extremity—his inculpation of society comes so near to being absolute that it is experienced as an exhilarating liberation, if not, alas, from the bondage of social necessity, then at least from the duress of its moral authority.

This being so, there will be no ready disposition to accept a view of the mind in its relation to society which proposes the idea that authenticity is exactly the product of the prescriptions of society and depends upon these prescriptions being kept in force. Such a view has been advanced, and not by some conservative humanist but by a writer whose own inculpation of society is scarcely mild, by none other than Herbert Marcuse. It is not a view that Marcuse intended to adopt. To all appearance, it forced itself upon him in the course of his putting forward a quite opposite view. The contradiction that thus manifests itself in *Eros and Civilization* is confusing when it first turns up, and Marcuse, so far as I can discern, never resolves it, yet the muddle it makes of his argument is to the credit of his honesty.

Eros and Civilization is Marcuse's attempt to bring Marx and Freud into harmony with each other. As its title suggests, it directly confronts the doctrine of *Civilization and Its Discontents*. Like Norman O. Brown, whose *Life Against Death* has certain affinities with *Eros and Civilization*,[1] Marcuse holds Freud's book in high regard, and he, like Brown, deals rigorously with the liberal revisionists of Freudian doctrine, such as Erich Fromm, who seek to bring into question the premises of its pessimism. Marcuse, accepting these premises, undertakes to refute the outcome of the argument which Freud develops from them, the conclusion that the structure of the mind cannot be altered or its distress significantly reduced.

Marcuse's belief in the possibility of a radical change in the mental organization rests upon his claim that quite considerable changes have in fact already taken place in the quarter-century since the publication of *Civilization and Its Discontents*. Advances in technology and developments in the economy, Marcuse says, have reduced the imperative force of material necessity which played so important a part in Freud's account of the development of the mind of man in civilization. As a consequence, the inhibition and constraint which necessity entails are measurably less exigent. The general relaxation of moral restriction has had a discernible effect upon the individual psyche, to the extent of having brought about an alteration of its very structure. The change that Marcuse believes already to have occurred he takes to be the earnest of more momentous changes to

---

[1] *Eros and Civilization* appeared in 1955, *Life Against Death* in 1959. Brown in his Preface speaks of Marcuse's book as taking the same direction as his own—that is, towards reopening 'the possibility of the abolition of repression'.

come. He foresees that the imperative and coercive nature of the superego, which he indicates by his terms 'surplus repression' and 'performance principle', will become obsolete—his projected curve of ensuing mental change points to the end of 'alienation', to the realization of the young Marx's envisioned state of freedom in which all human activity is gratuitous.

Marcuse addresses himself specifically and uncompromisingly to the two criteria by which Freud appraises the mental health of an individual, that is to say, his chances of living in civilization with a minimum of unhappiness or with a maximum of compensating gratification. These criteria are the ability to work and the full development of genital sexuality. In both there is doubtless to be discerned a degree, or a kind, of personal liberty. The ability to work presumably implies the desire to work; Freud scarcely had in mind enforced labour, rather a purposive and constructive activity which holds out the promise of satisfaction. And the development of genital sexuality can be said to have succeeded only if it realizes itself in autonomy and pleasure. Yet of course both genital sexuality and work imply a considerable degree of constraint and renunciation. In the present condition of humanity the most freely chosen and best-loved work involves frustration and requires pertinacity and self-discipline. And the development of genital sexuality is an arduous process which fulfils itself only through the renunciation of earlier modes of sexual gratification. Marcuse, whose prophetic range extends to envisaging an eventual triumph over death, or at least over all fear of death, foresees the day when the 'performance principle', which came into being at the behest of the superego and which at present determines both our conception of work and the imperativeness of the ideal of genital sexuality, will surrender its

stern rule. In the spirit of William Blake, Marcuse characterizes the phallus as an agent of alienation and tyranny—
Blake calls it 'a pompous High Priest' whose insistence that
it enter 'by a secret place' denies that the body is holy in
'every Minute Particular'. When the infantile sexual impulses, those which Freud calls polymorphous-perverse,
are no longer repressed in favour of an exclusive genitality,
the circuit of renunciation and guilt will be broken and
the death-instinct, which is established in the superego,
will be deprived of its energy of aggression against the
self.

Thus the movement of Marcuse's argument, on its way
towards the destiny of peace, freedom, and pleasure which
has been made feasible by the reduction of material necessity and the cultural constraints it entails. But, as I have
said, at one point in its course the argument diverges into
a startling negation of itself. It suddenly is made plain that
the relaxation of moral restrictions which is to be observed
in the American culture of 1955, when Marcuse wrote,
and which is said to license the hope of a redeeming psychic
mutation, does not in itself give Marcuse any satisfaction.
On the contrary, he regards it with a dismay which he
explains in considerable detail.

The chief cause of Marcuse's distress is what follows
from the alteration of the traditional role of the family,
which has become so much less decisive in the rearing of
the child that the morphology of the psyche is no longer
what Freud described it to be. Marcuse is here far from
insisting on the harm done to the ego by the gratuitous
severity, the 'surplus repression', of the superego as it was
classically brought into being by the family. Quite the
opposite: his whole concern is with the devolution of the
power of the superego, which he sees as resulting in a
deplorably lowered degree of individuality and autonomy.

'Through the struggle with mother and father as the targets of love and aggression,' he says, 'the younger generation entered societal life with impulses, ideas, and needs which were largely *their own*. Consequently, the formation of the superego, the repressive modifications of their impulses, their renunciation and sublimation were very personal experiences. Precisely because of this, their adjustment left painful scars and life . . . still retained a sphere of private nonconformity.' But in our contemporary cultural situation, Marcuse says, with the authority of the family, especially of the father, much diminished, the individual's ego 'has shrunk to such a degree that the multiform antagonistic processes between id, ego, and superego cannot unfold themselves in their classic form'. In the present dispensation 'the formation of the mature ego seems to skip the stage of individualization', with the result that 'the generic atom becomes directly a social atom'.

What Marcuse is saying about the development of the individual we have heard before: he means exactly what Rousseau meant when he spoke of the 'sentiment of being' which socialization invades and negates. Rousseau's sense of the attenuated sentiment of being of his contemporaries as compared with that of the ancient Spartans, or of the Parisians as compared with the Genevans, is paralleled by Marcuse's preference for the personalitytype shaped by a relatively repressive society, such as Freud took for granted, as against the personalitytype of a later, more permissive day.

Expectably enough, the adverse political implications of reduced individuality are of the first importance for Marcuse. He is apprehensive that, as compared with a traditional society, an affluent, permissive, and pleasureoriented society will control the individual both more efficiently and more profoundly, and he is constrained to conclude that moral intransigence and political activism are brought into being by renunciation and sublimation. But it is not only for moral and political reasons that Marcuse, in the face of his Utopian commitment, prefers the character-structure shaped by a non-permissive society. His judgement in this matter, like Rousseau's, is in some part directed by what I have called an aesthetic of personality. He *likes* people to have 'character', cost what it may in frustration. He holds fast to the belief that the right quality of human life, its intensity, its creativity, its felt actuality, its weightiness, requires the stimulus of exigence. It is a certitude which is in firm accord with the prevailing ethical style of the century in which Marcuse was born. In 1819 Keats said in one of his most memorable letters, 'Do you not see how necessary a World of Pains and troubles is to school an Intelligence and make it a soul?', that is to say, an ego or self which, as he puts it, is *'destined to possess the sense of Identity'*. (The emphasis is Keats's.) Freud, as we have seen, in his own wry way imputed to necessity the same developmental function. And Marcuse, in the very act of prophesying the virtual end of necessity, discovers in it a perverse beneficence— upon its harsh imperative depends the authenticity of the individual and his experience.

No doubt there is some Hegelian device which will properly resolve the contradiction between Marcuse's predilection for the strongly defined character-structure that necessity entails and his polemical commitment to a Utopia which will do away with necessity. I have not been able to discover that this dialectical ingenuity has been brought into play. The contradiction is allowed to stand, together with the baffling question of how the process of Utopian redemption is to be carried forward on the ground of such psychic changes as Marcuse observed in 1955, which issued in a character-structure and a culture which in his view are as deficient in grace as in authenticity.

iv

I have suggested that, by the store which he puts upon a character-structure which is defined and strengthened by the demands of a traditional society, Marcuse sets himself apart from, and at odds with, the prevailing tendency of radical speculation about personal authenticity. The extent of his alienation may be measured by reference to an extreme though characteristic manifestation of this tendency which in recent years has come dramatically to the fore—the view that insanity is a state of being in which an especially high degree of authenticity inheres.

This remarkable opinion has developed, we may sup-pose, partly in response to the increasing overtness of mental illness in our epoch and the virulence of the form it takes. Some four decades ago psychoanalysts found it possible to observe that the hysterical neuroses with which Freud was concerned in his early practice and theory were giving way to the so-called character neuroses, whose symptoms were less overt and gross, chiefly anxieties and incapacities which, however painful they might be, did not typically have the effect of incapacitating the patient for social life. This leni-tive trend of pathology—or of the cognizance of pathology —would now seem to have reversed itself towards mental conditions which are more severe than neurosis of any kind. It is not neurosis which now preoccupies the attention of psychiatric theory, including that put forward by laymen, but the far more extreme pathology of psychosis, especially schizophrenia. The Freudian clinical theory is by no means to be written off as irrelevant to schizophrenia, but its characteristic therapeutic procedure is not decisively efficacious in the treatment of this pathology. As for the Freudian ethos, what I have called its patrician posture of simultaneous acceptance of and detachment from life in civilization makes it patently—and bitterly—inappropriate to the situation of the psychotic person.

Given the magnitude and the terrible pathos of the situation—it has been estimated that one out of every hundred children becomes schizophrenic—and given the inconclusiveness of attempts to locate the etiology of schizophrenia in one or another biological malfunction, it was inevitable that the cause of this grievous pathology should be sought in social factors. It was no less inevitable that, when once this causative connection had been established with any semblance of plausibility, the characterization of society that followed from it should be of an ultimately pejorative kind: society was to be thought of, not as civilization's agent exacting for the boon of human development a price that was high yet not finally beyond what the means of the race might afford, but as the destroyer of the very humanity it pretended to foster. What was not inevitable was that this line of thought should issue in the view that insanity is a state of human existence which is to be esteemed for its commanding authenticity.

The position is grounded on two assumptive reasons. One is that insanity is a direct and appropriate response to the coercive inauthenticity of society. That is to say, insanity is not only a condition inflicted by the demands of society and passively endured; it is also an act, expressing the intention of the insane person to meet and overcome the coercive situation; and whether or not it succeeds in this intention, it is at least an act of criticism which exposes the true nature of society—thus interpreted, insanity is said to be a form of rationality and it is society itself that stands under the imputation of being irrational to the point of insanity.

The second reason is that insanity is a negation of limiting conditions in general, a form of personal existence in which power is assured by self-sufficiency.

To deal with this phenomenon of our intellectual culture in the way of analytical argument would, I think, be supererogatory. The position may be characterized as being in an intellectual mode to which analytical argument is not appropriate. This is the intellectual mode that once went under the name of cant. The disappearance of the word from the modern vocabulary is worth remarking. In characteriz-ing the position as I do it is not my purpose to minimize its cultural significance, which, in fact, I take to be momentous.

It was almost though not quite cant that Norman O. Brown uttered when, in his Phi Beta Kappa address at Columbia University in 1960, he spoke of the 'blessing' and the 'supernatural powers' which he desired to attain and which, he said, came only with madness. Professor Brown was at pains to specify, with due reference to Socrates in the *Phaedrus* and to Ficino and Nietzsche, that the necessary madness must be 'holy' madness. That is to say, when he identified the state of imagination through which the individual escapes his bondage to social institu-tions and to the democratic form of reason which is established in science and, indeed, in language itself, he did not mean literal insanity, but only insanity in the virtually metaphorical sense which is commonly signalized by the use of the more genial word 'madness' and validated by its ancient provenance. But though this is not yet cant, it presses towards becoming that and it makes the way easier for such fully achieved cant as is to be seen in David Cooper's introduction to the English translation of Michel Foucault's book about the development of the modern conception of madness as a pathology, *Histoire de la folie*.

Dr. Cooper is a well-known polemical psychiatrist and has been one of Dr. Laing's collaborators. 'Madness', he says, 'has in our age become some sort of lost truth.' And he goes on, 'Madness, as Foucault makes so impressively clear in this remarkable book, is a way of seizing *in extremis* the racinating groundwork of the truth that underlies our more specific realization of what we are about. The truth of mad-ness is what madness is. What madness is is a form of vision that destroys itself by its own choice of oblivion in the face of existing forms of social tactics and strategy. Madness, for instance, is a matter of voicing the realization that I am (or you are) Christ.' So far from being an illness, a deprivation of any kind, madness is health fully realized at last. Laing has a better intelligence and a better prose than Cooper and can therefore be more qualified and complex. In his view it is only *'sometimes'* (the emphasis is his) that 'transcendental experiences . . . break through in psychosis' to show their relation 'to those experiences of the divine that are the living fount of all religion'. Laing distinguishes between ' "true" ' madness and such madness as is a 'travesty' of healing; only the ' "true" ' madness gives rise to transcendental experiences of heuristic value. Yet all psychosis is to be thought of as a process of therapy, not in itself a disease but an effort to cure a disease, and there can be no qualification of the certitude that 'true sanity entails in one way or another the dissolution of the normal ego, that false self completely adjusted to our alienated social reality. . . .'

Who that has had experience of our social reality will doubt its alienated condition? And who that has thought of his experience in the light of certain momentous specu-lations made over the last two centuries, of which a few have been touched on in these pages, will not be disposed to find some seed of cogency in a view that proposes an antinomian reversal of all accepted values, of all received realities?

But who that has spoken, or tried to speak, with a psychotic friend will consent to betray the masked pain of his bewilderment and solitude by making it the paradigm of liberation from the imprisoning falsehoods of an alien-ated social reality? Who that finds intelligible the sentences which describe madness (to use the word that cant prefers) in terms of transcendence and charisma will fail to pene-trate to the great refusal of human connection that they express, the appalling belief that human existence is made authentic by the possession of a power, or the persuasion of its possession, which is not to be qualified or restricted by the co-ordinate existence of any fellow man?

Yet the doctrine that madness is health, that madness is liberation and authenticity, receives a happy welcome from a consequential part of the educated public. And when we have given due weight to the likelihood that those who respond positively to the doctrine don't have it in mind to go mad, let alone insane—it is characteristic of the intellec-tual life of our culture that it fosters a form of assent which does not involve actual credence—we must yet take it to be significant of our circumstance that many among us find it gratifying to entertain the thought that alienation is to be overcome only by the completeness of alienation, and that alienation completed is not a deprivation or deficiency but a potency. Perhaps exactly because the thought is assented to so facilely, so without what used to be called seriousness, it might seem that no expression of disaffection from the social existence was ever so desperate as this eagerness to say that authenticity of personal being is achieved through an ultimate isolateness and through the power that this is presumed to bring. The falsities of an alienated social reality are rejected in favour of an upward psychopathic mobility to the point of divinity, each one of us a Christ—but with none of the inconveniences of undertaking to intercede, of being a sacrifice, of reasoning with rabbis, of making sermons, of having disciples, of going to weddings and to funerals, of beginning something and at a certain point remarking that it is finished.

REFERENCE NOTES

I. SINCERITY: ITS ORIGIN AND RISE

page

4   'Why is it . . . never made?'/ *The Letters of Charles Dickens*, ed. W. Dexter (Nonesuch Press, London, 1938), vol. ii, pp. 620–1.

5   'Below the surface-stream . . . feel indeed'/ *The Poetical Works of Matthew Arnold*, ed. C. B. Tinker and H. F. Lowry (O.U.P., London and New York, 1950), p. 483.

      'Every individual human being . . . this ideal'/ F. Schiller, *On the Aesthetic Education of Man*, ed. and trans. E. M. Wilkinson and L. A. Willoughby (Clarendon Press, Oxford, 1967), p. 17.

      'Be true! . . . be inferred'/ Nathaniel Hawthorne, *The Scarlet Letter*, ch. xxiv, 'Conclusion'.

7   'The aesthetic point of view . . . discussing my work'/ This statement, presumably quoted from a letter of Gide's to the author, is the epigraph on the title-page of *André Gide* by Jean Hytier, trans. R. Howard (Doubleday Anchor, Garden City, N.Y., 1962; Constable, London, 1963). Eliot's statement is made in 'Tradition and the Individual Talent' and Joyce's in ch. v of *A Portrait of the Artist as a Young Man*.

      'No literature . . . concerned with salvation'/ L. Trilling, 'On the Teaching of Modern Literature', *Beyond Culture* (Viking, New York; Secker, London, 1965), p. 8.

8   'A poem in which . . . a *persona* of the author's'/ D. Davie, 'On Sincerity: From Wordsworth to Ginsberg', *Encounter*, Oct. 1968, pp. 61–6.

page

10   *The Presentation of Self in Everyday Life*/ By Erving Goffman (New York, 1959; London, 1969).

11   'Those masterful images . . . the heart'/ W. B. Yeats, 'The Circus Animals' Desertion', *Collected Poems* (Macmillan, London and New York, 1956), p. 336. Copyright 1940 by Georgie Yeats, renewed 1968 by Bertha Georgie Yeats, Michael Yeats, and Anne Yeats. Quoted by permission of Mr. M. B. Yeats, Macmillan & Co. Ltd., The Macmillan Company, New York, and the Macmillan Company of Canada Ltd.

17–18 Of this Rousseau . . . 'vice and virtue'/ J.-J. Rousseau's *Lettre à M. d'Alembert sur les spectacles* (1758) has been translated by Allan Bloom as *Politics and the Arts: Letter to M. d'Alembert on the Theatre* (Free Press, Glencoe, Ill., 1960), and is quoted here by permission of The Macmillan Company. For Rousseau's discussion of Molière, see pp. 34–47.

19   *Culture and Society*/ By Raymond Williams (London and New York, 1958).

19–20 Frances Yates . . . Zevedei Barbu . . . Paul Delany . . . the new genre/ F. Yates, 'Bacon and the Menace of English Lit.', *New York Review of Books*, 27 March 1969, p. 37; Z. Barbu, *Problems of Historical Psychology* (Routledge, London; Grove Press, New York, 1960), p. 146; P. Delany, *British Autobiography in the Seventeenth Century* (Routledge, London; Columbia Univ. Press, New York, 1969), p. 19.

20   'the idiocy of village life'/ K. Marx and F. Engels, *The Communist Manifesto*, in *A Handbook of Marxism*, ed. E. Burns (Random House, New York; Martin Lawrence, London, 1935), p. 27.

21   Michael Walzer . . . ' "advanced" intellectuals . . .'/ M. Walzer, *The Revolution of the Saints* (Harvard Univ. Press, Cambridge, Mass., 1965; Weidenfeld, London, 1966), p. 121.

page

22 Castiglione's *Courtier* . . . not what it should be/ B. Castiglione, *The Book of the Courtier*, trans. C. S. Singleton (Doubleday Anchor, New York, 1959), pp. 287–95.

23 the writer cannot . . . as he was and is/ See, *passim*, Delany's admirable work previously cited.

24 Georges Gusdorf . . . internal space/ G. Gusdorf, 'Conditions et limites de l'autobiographie', in *Formen der Selbstdarstellung*, ed. Reichenkron and Haase (Berlin, 1956), p. 108.

 He did not . . . as an individual he was of consequence/ Delany, p. 11.

25 Jacques Lacan . . . the manufacture of mirrors/ J. Lacan, 'Le stade du miroir comme formateur de la fonction du Je, telle qu'elle nous est révélée dans l'expérience psychanalytique', *Revue française de psychanalyse*, vol. xiii (1949), pp. 449–55. The influence of mirrors in the development of the sense of individuality is touched on by Gusdorf, pp. 108–9, and by C. Hill, *The Century of Revolution*, p. 253.

 If he is an artist . . . threescore of them/ The correlation of mirrors, self-portraiture, and autobiography is made by Delany, pp. 12–14.

II. THE HONEST SOUL AND THE DISINTEGRATED CONSCIOUSNESS

28 Karl Marx . . . 'unique masterpiece' will give him/ *Selected Correspondence [of] Karl Marx and Friedrich Engels*, trans. D. Torr (International Publishers, New York, 1942), pp. 259–61. For the original letter, with its amusing 'Ich finde heute by accident, dass zwei "*Neveu de Rameau*". . .' and '. . . sagt old Hegel darüber . . .'. See *Karl Marx–Friedrich Engels Werke* (Dietz, Berlin, 1965), vol. xxxii, pp. 303–4.

 'If your little savage . . . sleep with his mother' / I quote from the translation by Jacques Barzun in *Diderot: 'Rameau's Nephew' and*

28   *Other Works*, ed. R. Bowen (Bobbs-Merrill, Indianapolis,
         1964), pp. 8–87, by permission of Doubleday & Co. Inc. I
         have found useful E. J. Geary's edition of *Le Neveu de Rameau*
         (Integral Editions, n.d., dist. Schoenhof, Cambridge, Mass.).
         For the occasions of Freud's quotation of the passage see the
         editorial note on p. 338 of vol. xvi (*Introductory Lectures on
         Psychoanalysis*) of the Standard Edition of *The Complete Psycho-
         logical Works of Sigmund Freud* (Hogarth Press, London, 1963).

30   The words, of course, are . . . Pascal's / *Pensées* No. 258 in the
         arrangement of H. F. Stewart's bi-lingual edition (Routledge,
         London; Pantheon, New York, 1950), p. 150. I have used
         Stewart's text but not his translation.

         'the first modern man' / L. Goldmann, *The Hidden God*
         (Routledge, London; Humanities Press, New York, 1964),
         p. 171 et seq.

34   such words as 'nobility' . . . 'heroism of flattery' / I quote from
         J. B. Baillie's translation of *The Phenomenology of Mind*, rev. and
         corr. 2nd ed. (Allen & Unwin, London, 1949; Harper, New
         York, 1967), pp. 509–48.

49   the 'magic of nobility' / F. Kermode, introduction to *The
         Tempest*, Arden Edition (Methuen, London; Harvard Univ.
         Press, Cambridge, Mass., 1961), p. liv.

         'I don't know . . . attach themselves to me'/ I have used the
         translation by Harry Steinhauer in his bi-lingual edition: J. W.
         von Goethe, *The Sorrows of Young Werther* (Bantam, New
         York, 1962).

III. THE SENTIMENT OF BEING AND THE SENTIMENTS OF ART

55   'The image of the self . . . effaced from the universe . . .'/ W.
         Sypher, *Loss of Self in Modern Literature and Art* (Vintage,
         New York, 1964), p. 15. The 'idea of the self we have not only
         rejected but destroyed' is identified as having been created by
         the 'romantic-liberal tradition' (p. 8).

page

56   Anna Freud . . . no attempt to explain it / A. Freud, *Some Difficulties in the Path of Psychoanalysis* (International Universities Press, New York, 1969).

57   Henri Peyre . . . that the French have shown / *Literature and Sincerity* (Yale Univ. Press, New Haven and London, 1963), p. 1.

58   'I have resolved . . . will be myself'/ I have used J. M. Cohen's translation: *The Confessions of J.-J. Rousseau* (Penguin, Baltimore and Harmondsworth, 1953).

60   'they make men . . . worthy of their mutual approval'/ a 'uniform and false veil . . . enlightenment of our century'/ J.-J. Rousseau, *The First and Second Discourses*, ed. R. D. Masters, trans. R. D. and J. R. Masters (St. Martins Press, New York, 1964), pp. 35, 38.

62   'The savage lives . . . sentiment of his own being'/ Rousseau, *First and Second Discourses*, p. 179.

63   The general effect . . . 'new energy to all the passions'/ 'Is it possible . . . intemperate and mad?'/ 'I suspect . . . than at the end' / Rousseau, *Politics and the Arts*, p. 20.

64   'When a man has gone . . . has just rendered it?' / the art of 'counterfeiting himself . . . another character than his own' / *Politics and the Arts*, p. 25.

65   'What!', he asks . . . 'there ought to be many . . .'/ 'People think . . . at the expense of the living' / In the place of 'exclusive entertainments . . . loves himself in the others'/ *Politics and the Arts*, pp. 17, 125–6.

66   'Rousseau at his most unpleasant' / P. Gay, *The Party of Humanity* (Knopf, New York; Weidenfeld, London, 1964), p. 250.

66   the 'other-directed' personality / D. Riesman, in collaboration
        with R. Denny and N. Glazer, *The Lonely Crowd: A Study in
        the Changing American Character* (Yale Univ. Press, New Haven
        and London, 1950). For the definition of 'other-directed' see
        p. 19.

68   'he fills only . . . in his own name'/ Rousseau, *Politics and the Arts*,
        p. 15.

        'the unbroken sentiment of his being'/ Rousseau, *Confessions*,
        p. 19.

68–9   'he was as sincere . . . Jean-Jacques Rousseau'/ J. M. Thompson,
        Robespierre (O.U.P., London, 1939), p. 280.

69   the 'profound sincerity . . . subjugated the Assembly' / A.
        Mathiez, *The French Revolution*, trans. C. A. Phillips (Knopf,
        New York, 1928), p. 462.

69–70   'enacted the Revolution'/'to tear the mask . . . off the face of
        French society' / The Revolution . . . man's unknowable heart/
        H. Arendt, *On Revolution* (Viking, New York, 1963; Faber,
        London, 1964), pp. 85–110, esp. pp. 101–2.

72   Jane Austen . . . beyond this one work/ See F. W. Bradbrook,
        Jane Austen and Her Predecessors (C.U.P., Cambridge, 1966),
        p. 121.

72–3   'From this common taste . . . than of being so' / Rousseau,
        Politics and the Arts, p. 82.

73   'a contentment and peace . . . sweet and dear'/ Rousseau,
        Rêveries V, Pléiade Edition, vol. i, p. 1047, quoted by R. D.
        Masters, *The Political Philosophy of Rousseau* (Princeton Univ.
        Press, Princeton and London, 1968), p. 98.

74–5   'My expectations . . . I required no more'/Rousseau, *Confessions*,
        p. 52.

IV. THE HEROIC, THE BEAUTIFUL, THE AUTHENTIC

page

81–2   'Even as a unit . . . progressive states of mind. . . .' / *The North British Review*, lii, April 1870, pp. 129–52.

84   Jacques Barzun says . . . 'made war on two things—our culture and the heroic' / Mr. Barzun acknowledges the statement to be his, although he is as little able as I am to recall where he made it.

Story-telling . . . the end it has in view is 'wisdom' / W. Benjamin, 'The Storyteller: Reflections on the Works of Nikolai Leskov', *Illuminations*, ed. H. Arendt, trans. H. Zahn (Harcourt, Brace, New York, 1968; Cape, London, 1970), pp. 86–7.

'A hero is one who looks like a hero' / R. Warshow, 'The Westerner', *The Immediate Experience* (Doubleday, Garden City, N.Y., 1962), p. 153.

. . . the hero is an actor / M. Bieber, *The History of the Greek and Roman Theatre*, 1st ed. (Princeton Univ. Press, Princeton and London, 1939), p. 15.

86   ' "To play one's part" . . . The actors . . . are their own audience' / H. Jonas, *The Gnostic Religion*, 2nd ed. rev. (Beacon Press, Boston, 1963), p. 249.

90   It is Wordsworth . . . 'best deserves [the] word "genius" ' / *Letters of James Joyce*, vols. ii and iii, ed. R. Ellmann (Faber, London; Viking, New York, 1966), vol. ii, p. 91.

91   'What is brought forward? . . . the most naked simplicity possible' / Letter of 14 June 1802, *The Early Letters of William and Dorothy Wordsworth*, ed. E. de Selincourt (Clarendon Press, Oxford, 1935), p. 306.

95   Beauty, it tells us . . . 'an inward sense of melting and languor' / E. Burke, *A Philosophical Enquiry into the Origin of our Ideas of the Sublime and the Beautiful*, ed. J. T. Boulton (Routledge, London; Columbia Univ. Press, New York, 1958), pp. 149–50.

page
96   beauty has two modes . . . 'elasticity and power of prompt
        action' / 'The man who lives . . . from the state of savagery'/
        Schiller, *On the Aesthetic Education of Man*, pp. 113, 115.

97   The sublime does not please . . . 'grateful to the human mind'/
        Burke, *A Philosophical Enquiry*, pp. 50–1.

100   a story which will . . . 'make people ashamed of their existence'/
        J.-P. Sartre, *Nausea*, trans. L. Alexander (Hamilton, London,
        1962; New Directions, New York, 1964), p. 237.

        'We all remember . . . based on the most platitudinous of con-
        ventions' / N. Sarraute, 'Flaubert', trans. M. Jolas, *Partisan
        Review*, Spring 1966, p. 203.

102-3   'a protoplasmic vision . . . the incarnation of everybody'/ J.-P.
        Sartre, introduction to N. Sarraute, *Portrait of a Man Unknown*,
        trans. M. Jolas (Braziller, New York, 1958), pp. xii, ix.

V. SOCIETY AND AUTHENTICITY

112   'We will not have to do . . . where it will'/'English believes . . .
        rests on their national sincerity'/R. W. Emerson, *English Traits*,
        ed. H. M. Jones (Harvard Univ. Press, Cambridge, Mass.
        1966), pp. 76, 70.

117   This assumption . . . 'with the religious system' / S. Freud,
        Civilization and Its Discontents (*The Complete Psychological Works
        of Sigmund Freud*, Standard Edition, vol. xxi) (Hogarth Press,
        London, 1961), p. 76.

        'Never, perhaps, . . . awful with inscrutable fate'/ F. W. H.
        Myers, 'George Eliot', *Essays, Classical and Modern* (Macmillan,
        London, 1921), p. 495.

118   'The first duty in life . . . has yet discovered' / O. Wilde,
        'Phrases and Philosophies for the Use of the Young', *The
        Artist as Critic: Critical Writings of Oscar Wilde*, ed. R. Ellmann
        (Random House, New York, 1969; W. H. Allen, London,
        1970), p. 433.

page

119   'Man is least himself . . . tell you the truth'/Wilde, 'The Critic as Artist: A Dialogue, Part II', *The Artist as Critic*, p. 389.

'There is no . . . the sincerest man'/'Many men can . . . for themselves'/ R. W. Emerson, *The Journals and Miscellaneous Notebooks*, ed. A. W. Plumstead and H. Hayford (Harvard Univ. Press, Cambridge, Mass., 1969), vol. iii, p. 423; *Letters and Social Aims* (*Complete Works*, Centenary Edition, vol. viii) (Houghton Mifflin, Boston and New York, 1904), p. 196.

119-20   'Every profound spirit needs a mask'/'It seems . . . Platonism in Europe'/ F. Nietzsche, *Beyond Good and Evil*, trans. Walter Kaufmann (Vintage, New York, 1966), pp. 51, 3.

120   '. . . In art there is . . . the truths of masks'/Wilde, 'The Truth of Masks', *The Artist as Critic*, p. 432.

121   Schiller has in mind . . . 'the earnestness of duty and destiny'/ 'Man only plays . . . a human being when he plays'/ Schiller, *On the Aesthetic Education of Man*, p. 107.

122-3   'The less you eat . . . the more you *have*'/'The less you *are* . . . to buy itself . . .'/ K. Marx, *Early Writings*, ed. and trans. T. B. Bottomore (Watts, London, 1963; McGraw-Hill, New York, 1964), pp. 171-2. Quoted by permission of Pitman Publishing and the McGraw-Hill Book Company.

124   'If I have no money . . . an *effective* vocation'/'Let us assume man . . . your *real individual* life'/ Marx, *Early Writings*, pp. 192-3, 193-4.

125-6   'They require you to be . . . hardly even thought is free'/Emerson, *English Traits*, pp. 66-7.

128   'If there is a test . . . *ce déplorable Ruskin*'/R. Banham, *Theory and Design in the First Machine Age*, 2nd ed. (Praeger, New York, 1967; Architectural Press, London, 1970), p. 12.

129   'When, then,' he demanded . . . 'who has now grown old . . .'/

page

129   F. T. Marinetti, quoted by Banham, *Theory and Design in the First Machine Age*, p. 123.

a 'prosthetic God'/Freud, *Civilization and Its Discontents*, p. 92.

129–30   The fifth proposition . . . 'through the centre of the earth'/ Banham, *Theory and Design in the First Machine Age*, p. 103.

VI. THE AUTHENTIC UNCONSCIOUS

135   Benjamin speaks . . . 'an old-fashioned ring'/Benjamin, 'The Storyteller: Reflections on the Works of Nikolai Leskov', *Illuminations*, p. 86.

Richard Gilman . . . 'a blueprint, a lesson'/R. Gilman, *The Confusion of Realms* (Random House, New York, 1969; Weidenfeld, London, 1970), p. 78.

136–7   It is a multiplicity . . . 'an organism or structure'/'a task properly completed . . . at worst meretricious' / 'Without a sense . . . satisfactory history'/G. R. Elton, *Political History: Principles and Practice* (Basic Books, New York; A. Lane, London, 1970), pp. 158–9, 161.

137   'Industrial society . . . of nostalgia, of sentimentality'/Its coming to the verge . . . 'the titanic struggle against Hitler'/'A narrative past . . . with sharp and positive beginnings'/J. H. Plumb, *The Death of the Past* (Macmillan, London, 1969; Houghton Mifflin, Boston, 1970), pp. 14–15, 86, 77.

138   Nietzsche says . . . all things, and man himself, seem 'weightless'/ Quoted by K. Jaspers, *Nietzsche and Christianity*, trans. E. B. Ashton (Regnery, Chicago, 1961), p. 14, from *Nachgelassen Werke, Nietzsches Werke,* ed. Elisabeth Förster-Nietzsche (Leipzig, 1903), vol. xiii, pp. 316–17.

'To write the History of England . . . considerable in the world!'/ T. Carlyle, 'Shooting Niagara: And After?', *Scottish and Other Miscellanies* (Dent, London; Dutton, New York, 1932), p. 321.

page

141 This is the disposition of mind . . . 'the uncovering of underlying truth' / H. F. Ellenberger, *The Discovery of the Unconscious: History and Evolution of a Dynamic Psychiatry* (Basic Books, New York; A. Lane, London, 1970), p. 537.

142 'a kind of façade for the id'/Freud, *Civilization and Its Discontents*, p. 66.

143 'We are all ill'/ S. Freud, *Introductory Lectures on Psychoanalysis* (Part III) (Standard Edition, vol. xvi) (Hogarth Press, London, 1963), p. 358.

144–5 'By the distinction . . . cut the psychic whole into two'/'I am the ego . . . their conscious reality'/'I am not these psychic facts . . . an external phenomenon'/J.-P. Sartre, *Being and Nothingness: An Essay on Phenomenological Ontology*, trans. H. E. Barnes (Philosophical Library, New York, 1956; Methuen, London, 1969), pp. 50, 51.

146–7 '. . . It is not enough . . . in order not to be conscious of it'/ Sartre, *Being and Nothingness*, pp. 52–3.

147 'There is something in the ego . . . before it is made conscious'/ S. Freud, *The Ego and the Id* (Standard Edition, vol. xix) (Hogarth Press, London, 1961), p. 17.

148 What is more . . . 'to some extent its headquarters' / Freud, *Civilization and Its Discontents*, pp. 66, 118.

To Freud's surprise . . . 'extremely high ones'/ Freud, *The Ego and the Id*, p. 26.

153 'It is in keeping . . . external measures of coercion' / S. Freud, *The Future of an Illusion* (Standard Edition, vol. xxi) (Hogarth Press, London, 1961), p. 11.

158 '*Mit welchem Recht?*' . . ./ The anecdote is, I fear, the fruit of a faulty memory. Actually Freud flared out in the manner described

on quite a different occasion. Ernest Jones relates that in 1923, when Freud's closest and most devoted associates understood that a major operation was necessary to deal with his cancer, they debated whether or not Freud should be fully informed of this state of affairs. Many years later, when Freud had settled in London, Jones told him of the discussion and it was then that Freud used the angry phrase I quote. See Ernest Jones, *The Life and Work of Sigmund Freud,* vol. iii (Hogarth Press, London; Basic Books, New York, 1957), p. 93. I have let the error stand as essentially true. For Freud's refusal to take any drug stronger than aspirin, see Jones, p. 245: ' "I prefer to think in torment than not to be able to think clearly," he said.'

158–9 'the appropriation of human reality . . . enjoyment of the self for man'/Marx, *Early Writings*, p. 159.

160 'ontological insecurity'/R. D. Laing, *The Divided Self*, 2nd ed. (Penguin Books, Harmondsworth, 1961), p. 39 et seq.

It is the family . . . 'an unlivable situation'/R. D. Laing, *The Politics of Experience* (Penguin Books, Harmondsworth; Ballantine Books, New York, 1967), p. 115. See R. D. Laing and A. Esterson, *Sanity, Madness and the Family* (1970).

163 his terms 'surplus repression' and 'performance principle' / H. Marcuse, *Eros and Civilization* (Beacon Press, Boston, 1955; A. Lane, London, 1969), pp. 35, 37 f., 44 f.

165 'Through the struggle with mother . . . private nonconformity'/ But in our contemporary cultural situation . . . 'directly a social atom'/Marcuse, *Eros and Civilization*, pp. 96–7.

169 Professor Brown was at pains to specify . . . must be a 'holy' madness / N. O. Brown, 'Apocalypse', *Harper's Magazine*, May 1961, pp. 46–9.

170 'Madness', he says . . . 'that I am (or you are) Christ'/ D. Cooper, introduction to M. Foucault, *Madness and Civilization: A History of Insanity in the Age of Reason*, trans. R. Howard (Random House, New York, 1965; Tavistock, London, 1967), pp. vii–ix.

INDEX OF NAMES